RAIDERS AND HORSE THIEVES

Memoir of a Central Texas Baby Boomer

Jackie Ellis Stewart

Texas Review Press
Huntsville, Texas

FIRST EDITION

Requests for permission to acknowledge material from this work should be sent to:
Permissions
Texas Review Press
English Department
Sam Houston State University
Huntsville, TX 77341-2146

ACKNOWLEDGEMENTS:
It would not have been possible to write this account without the cooperation and collaborative efforts of my brother Joe Ellis, his wife, Judy, my sister Joy Wittera, and her husband Larry.

Suzanne Lieurance was instrumental in teaching me how to structure my story. Roger Boylan, my editor, who said to not worry about poor punctuation, "That's what I do." He also inspired me to continue writing and to publish this for the public rather than privately for family.

Special credit goes to Hal Jaffe of Jaffe Studio in Memphis, Tennessee, who granted Sam Houston State special dispensation to use a recent photograph he'd taken of me in this project. Anthony Cinciolo deserves special recognition for his unique definition of a family.

Thanks to my friends, Jenny Pinkowski, Aris Chafetz and Jean Gray who patiently suffered through way too many readings of the rough draft. I hope the wine helped.

My husband, Jack Stewart, deserves particular recognition for living with me while I wrote. It was one thing to remember individual instances and quite another to see them strung together. Jack is also the one who demanded I get this published as a tribute to Mother.

I sincerely appreciate the opportunity Dr. Paul Ruffin and his staff at Sam Houston State University have given me.

Jackie Ellis Stewart
Fall, 2015

Cover Design: Nancy Parsons, Graphic Design Group

Library of Congress Cataloging-in-Publication Data

Stewart, Jackie Ellis, 1946- author.
  Raiders and horse thieves : memoir of a Central Texas baby boomer / Jackie Ellis Stewart. -- First edition.
    pages cm
  ISBN 978-1-68003-061-7 (pbk. : alk. paper)
  1. Stewart, Jackie Ellis, 1946---Childhood and youth. 2. Women authors--Texas--Bastrop County--Biography. 3. Authors--Texas--Bastrop County--Biography. 4. Bastrop County (Tex.)--History--20th century. 5. Bastrop County (Tex.)--Biography--20th century. 6. Country life--Texas--Bastrop County--History--20th century. 7. Texas--Rural conditions. I. Title.
  F392.B23S74 2015
  976.4'32--dc23
                    2015018645

In loving memory of Virginia Lee McDaniel Ellis.
(1926-1978)

Contents

INTRODUCTION

It's in the Genes

We met about dawn at Joe and Judy's. My brother Joe and his wife are the last of our branch of the family still residing within the boundaries of our old home place. Early in their marriage, they bought five acres from our paternal grandmother. It's hard to believe, but Granny had never liked her eldest grandson. She thought he looked and acted too much like his maternal grandfather. The men from our father and grandmother's generation made Granny agree to the sale. They used simple, almost brutal words of one and two syllables to point out the necessity of having a family member close at hand in her dotage.

A second cousin instigated this expedition to Gonzales, in south-central Texas, in search of our ancestor, Absalom Ellis. He and his wife arrived almost on our heels. Although I hadn't seen him in over thirty years, his greeting was casual, with a one-armed hug as though he'd recently run into me at the grocery. A great-aunt and her daughter, another Ellis cousin, were the last to arrive.

It had rained during the night, and we watched the mist give way to the rising sun as we caravanned to our destination. I had flown in from Memphis the day before and was riding with my sister Joy. On these trips back home, I'm accustomed to riding from one place in the middle of nowhere to another. I'm not blessed with a sense of direction, and am always amazed when my brother and sister make their way intuitively along remote, unmarked country roads. This was no exception.

After an hour or so of driving, we finally reached our destination: an unremarkable wooden gate opening onto a cleared pasture. This was supposedly where Absalom Ellis, who came to Texas from Scotland, had lived and was buried.

Our cousin who organized this search had learned of the burial site from a descendant of another branch of our family who had visited the spot a number of years earlier. Our cousin tracked down the property owner and secured permission for us to pursue this genealogist's dream.

Our great-aunt was the only one who had given the trip some thought and planned ahead. She knows this family travels on its tummies and brought home-made chocolate-chip cookies. It's never too early or too late for a good cookie.

The rest of us were totally unprepared. It was muddy. One of us had worn wooden-soled flip-flop sandals and spent a good part of the morning pulling them out of the muck. Once we were through the gate, we realized the land was divided into two pastures by a barbed wire fence. A bull was confined on one side. Leary of this unfamiliar and potentially dangerous animal, I climbed through the barbed wire fence to explore the other half of the pasture.

It was Judy who found the family plot hidden among a clump of young mesquites. The larger headstone was broken; lying face down and embedded in the earth. A number of smaller markers had once surrounded it, but time and the weather, as well as grazing animals and invasive vegetation, had worn them down to indecipherable sandstone lumps. The men were able to pull the larger marker free; they used Joe's handkerchief to clean off the inscription. Sure enough: "Absalom Ellis."

We took snapshots of the worn stones and posed together to mark the occasion. Cookies were passed around in celebration. Some of us headed back home to tend to chores while the rest went out for more family bonding over a lunch of chicken-fried steak and pinto beans. Despite the excellent company and down-home comfort food, the experience left me feeling dissatisfied and frustrated.

We had validated Absalom's existence and filled a spot in the family tree, but who was he? I came away from the morning slightly disappointed. It had been a great family adventure, but I needed more than just a name on a weathered rock. I spent the rest of the trip visiting relatives and asking for details of our family history. No one knew much more than I, but one confirmed that we were of Scots-Irish descent and remarked, "Daddy was always fascinated by those people."

Back home, I researched the Scots-Irish and learned they have a long and flamboyant history. Early Roman records used the generic name Scoti or Scotti to describe the Irish who raided the coast of what was to become Scotland. They were described as raiders and horse thieves--stubborn and violent and private and poverty-stricken.

During the Great Famine, younger members of the family, girls as well as boys, made the trip across the ocean and sent money back to Ireland. Each one who left would send money back home for another family member to join them.

All the more desirable coastal land of the New World had been acquired by this time (the 1840s and '50s). The Scots-Irish entered this country through the Mid-Atlantic States rather than New England. Unsuccessful on all levels of life, these people merely wanted a place to live far away from any possible intervention from the government. Most appeared to lack any redeeming social graces, and any who tried to settle on the coast were encouraged one way or another to move further inland to the frontier. They settled first in Virginia and Maryland and then moved on to Kentucky. Some went further south from there, while others moved west.

I could almost hear the pieces of my family history click into place. The characteristics and attitudes attributed to the Scoti were still clearly evident in the people who surrounded me during my childhood. Their rough and ready qualities had evolved into the grandiose Texas attitude.

I came away with a new view of my lineage as a logical progression from Scoti raiders and horse thieves to the people and culture of my childhood.

Speed, little dreams, your winging
To that land across the sea
Where the Dinkey-Bird is singing
In the amfalula tree!

"The Dinkey-Bird"
By Eugene Fields

—CHAPTER ONE—

High Hopes and Good Intentions

I heard the brisk smack sound of wood hitting wood immediately followed by the light ping of a small bell. Muffled giggles and a light, quick shuffling followed.

It was chilly in my corner of the room, but Mother had covered me with several layers of blankets and securely tucked them around me. Curled on my side with my cheek cradled in the palm of one hand, I was deep in the dreamless sleep only a toddler can know.

The smacking, pinging, giggling routine started again. This time it was punctuated by the yip of a small dog. Curiosity pulled me from my warm slumbers. I rolled over and through the bars of my crib saw a magical sight.

We lived in a crudely constructed and rudely used one-room house set in a remote back pasture of central Texas. The ceiling was sheet rocked and the walls hung with boldly flowered but stained and torn wallpaper. The walls were badly scarred, and there were two or three gaping holes in the ceiling. The house had obviously set empty for a long time, or had been used for the storage of feed and grain.

It was the lighting that gave the scene a fanciful air. I was accustomed to the room being lighted by a single glaring bulb that hung from a wire in the middle of the room. At night, now and again, I would see the room partially illuminated by flashlight as Mother moved about, but it was now bathed in a soft flickering glow from the fireplace. A scraggly cedar tree hung with lights and tin foil stars stood adjacent. A tree in the house!

My father knelt in front of the tree. He held a simple C-shaped pound-a-peg toy at an extreme angle to the floor and smacked the peg briskly through the hole with enough force for it to ricochet off the bell and shoot across the room to hit Mother.

She stood barefoot in a flannel nightgown in front of the stove stirring a pot of oatmeal. Her reddish-brown hair was in two long braids that crossed at the nape of her neck and were pinned in a circle around her head.

Both of my parents laughed as she dodged the pegs and tended her pot. A white terrier-mix puppy with a black and brown face chased the pegs as they landed.

"Now look what you've done. The baby's awake," Mother said.

My father selected yet another peg to propel across the room. "It's time for her to get up and see what Santa brought." he replied.

"I know," answered my mother. "It's just that neither of us has slept all that well since the snake fell out of the ceiling. I find myself checking on her with the flashlight all through the night."

"Spotty, come here," called my father. The puppy obeyed and rolled over for a tummy rub. Patting the dog, he said, "I know it ain't easy, Dumple, but we're making good progress. I think we'll have a better chance of improving our finances by moving to the Holcomb Place. The house is a little bigger and sturdier. We'll be settled there about the time the new baby comes. We also have this fine watchdog to protect us all." Spotty was small enough to fit in my father's cupped hands. If she barked too hard, she would lose her balance and fall over.

Mother removed the pot from the flame. My father crossed the room. She turned from the stove. They rocked back and forth in an embrace as he gently rubbed her bottom. She nuzzled her face in the hollow of his neck and, smiling, said, "It was a piece of Christmas luck when you found that box of puppies abandoned alongside the road. We made three other families happy, and this one is already almost completely housebroken. She's as good as can be with Jackie Lee. I'm just not sure how we're going to afford to have her spayed."

"Oh, things always have a way of working out. Like the extra money you earned pulling the load of wild broom weeds for the florist. It only took a couple of weeks for the blisters and cuts on your hands to heal." He grinned and patted her rump.

She withdrew from him and turned to my crib, where I was about to clamber over the top. She lifted me out and set me on my feet to toddle across the cracked linoleum to my highchair by the table. It was December 25, 1948. In mid-April, I would be three.

I clearly remember being enthralled with my scrawny, youthful parents celebrating the holiday in a glow of optimism, love, and good cheer. I have no clear recollection of anyone sitting down with me to explain the differences between the male and female roles in our family, but before the next baby was born, I was already aware of them. The lessons I learned regarding "my place" were subtly taught and left no memory.

I knew my father was not comfortable being alone with me. My requests to accompany him on short excursions were turned down because I was a girl. My place was at home with Mother.

My relationship with my father was always strained. Mother said the first time he hit me was when we lived in this ramshackle house. I was curled on my tummy in the crib and crying. He felt I was taking too long to fall asleep and spanked me.

My memory fades for a while and opens again on a scene that must have taken place the following spring.

The Holcomb Place

My father used the money he had saved from serving in the Navy during World War II to purchase the Holcomb

Place—in the local dialect, "the Hawcum Place." My memory fails me here: I'm not certain if it was 250 or 500 acres, but it doesn't really matter. My parents were satisfied that it was an adequate beginning for my father's career as a cattleman, in his family's tradition, surrounded by his relatives.

He bought it from his maternal uncle, T.C. Watts. His maternal grandmother, Jesse Watts, lived on the homestead nearby that had been established by her husband Perry. The one-lane gravel road meandering past our front gate was Watts Lane. A large section of the property adjoining the Holcomb Place was part of Great-Granddaddy Watts' homestead.

My second memory is of playing on the rough wooden floor of a long, narrow, screened porch while Great-Granny Watts, standing in the door from the hall to the porch, called out, "Ginny and Gordon have just pulled up out front. Jackie Lee, go out on the front porch and see the special surprise your mother has for you."

I went through the house, and as I opened the front door, I saw Mother coming down the brick walk wreathed in smiles. She clutched a blanketed bundle to her chest. My father walked behind her carrying a suitcase. Mother bent down in front of me and said, "This is your new brother, Danny Joe."

I followed her into the house where she laid the baby on the bed in the front room and pulled the blanket down for me to get a better view. The baby responded to the cooler air by stretching and moving his arms. "Oh, look," I exclaimed, "He moves just like an egg beater." I recall saying this and the laughter it brought from the adults. I instantly loved my little brother.

My Father's Parents

For the next few days, we stayed at Great-Granny's to give Mother some time to recuperate a bit before we moved to the Holcomb Place. Our father's parents, J.C. and Zula Ellis, lived with Great-Granny Jesse Watts.

Zula Watts Ellis was cantankerous. Time spent in her company was always difficult. She treated Mother with great disdain and made no attempt to conceal her disapproval of our parents' marriage. My mother's parents were divorced. Her father was an alcoholic. My mother's mother relished her reputation as a "good ole girl" who liked to drink and dance and "carry on" with men who weren't her husband. Mother tried to win her mother-in-law's approval by being overly conscientious as a mother and wife.

It was an easy move to the Holcomb Place. Everything we owned fit in the back of the pickup. Our collection of household goods included a crib and two beds, a battered sofa, a small square kitchen table with several layers of chipped paint, four mismatched chairs, and a small radio. The tiny refrigerator and gas-cooking stove may already have been in the house. A swing hung on the screened front porch.

Early one morning, soon after the move, I was playing on the front porch while Mother worked at the back of the house. A pickup came down the hill and stopped at the edge of the stock tank just beyond the barn in front of our house. Granddaddy Ellis, my father's father, stepped out of the truck, one arm in a sling. He pulled a shovel from the back and walked to the edge of the stock tank. He strolled along the edge closest to the house for a while and then began to dig.

Mother rushed past me with Joe in her arms. "Jackie Lee, stay right here. Don't leave the porch. Butchie and Fido may be in the truck." These two dogs were his devoted, constant companions and invaluable for herding cattle, but threatening to small children.

I stood at the screened door, straining to hear the conversation between Mother and her father-in-law. I was too far away to hear what they were saying, but their body language was easily read. Mother didn't want her father-in-law out in the sun digging a ditch with a broken arm, but he was even more determined and won the dispute.

Water was a scarce commodity. There was a small cistern by the back of the house, but it was expensive and could only be used for drinking and cooking and bathing. Water was drawn from the stock tank and boiled for laundry. Mother was washing diapers on a scrub board for the new baby.

The pipe only had to be buried a few inches below the ground's surface to keep the livestock from tripping over it. Once it was laid, Mother could use the electric wringer-washing machine that sat on a concrete pad in the back yard.

Granddaddy was a little over six feet tall and probably weighed 140 pounds including his boots. He was a thinner, smaller-boned version of our father, right down to his cup-handle ears and curly black hair. The hard-headed determination he showed was typical of the men in my family, and all those of Scots-Irish descent in our community. Mother hovered around the front of the house the entire time he was digging to keep a close eye on him and provide him with a steady supply of cool water.

Our father's mother rarely visited us, even though we were less than five miles down the road. But Granddaddy Ellis dropped in regularly. What motivated him? Did Granddaddy do this digging to ease his own feelings of inadequacy, or did he realize his son was an inattentive spouse and he was trying to cover for him? Did it cause conflict between my paternal grandparents when Granddaddy was attentive to us and Mother? Our father was rarely home. The love and op-timistic good cheer of the previous Christmas seems to have waned somewhat under the drudgery of reality.

My Mother's Parents

It wasn't long after this episode that my mother's father made a brief appearance in our lives. "Jackie Lee!" Mother burst through the back door and stood on the porch to call me in from playing in the back yard. There was an exuberant ring to her voice.

"Hurry, come let me wash your face. We're about to have company. Your Grandpa McDaniel just phoned from Martin's General Store in Cedar Creek for directions. He'll be here in a few minutes."

Mother's father was tall, with a barrel chest and balding head. He wore rimless glasses. I sat on his lap while we sorted out family titles. "Since you already have a Granddaddy Ellis,

I will have to be your Grandpa McDaniel. That will keep things straight for us all," he reasoned.

I patted his shirtfront. "Momma says you used to have a pet white rat and would let him run around inside your shirt along your belt. Did you bring him with you?"

Grandpa McDaniel laughed. "No, I'm afraid he's gone to cheese heaven. Did your momma tell you about the time I had him in my shirt and the insurance salesman came to the door? I forgot about him being in there and was talking to the man when all of a sudden the salesman got a funny look and just left. I couldn't figure it out until I looked down. The rat had stuck his head out between two of my lower shirt buttons to join the conversation."

Mother and Grandpa laughed.

"Daddy," Mother said, "You always were bad about teasing strangers. I think the worst was when you told the census taker that you had three girls residing in your house."

"Well, I did," Grandpa said, with a note of mock indignation.

"No, Daddy," Mother scolded him. "You had one daughter and one stepdaughter living at home. That other 'girl' was Maw, your mother-in-law, who had to be over 70 at the time. You fibbed to the federal government."

Grandpa was quick to answer. "The federal government had no business asking about my household and personal life. Their nosey questions deserved exaggerated responses," he said, displaying that hardheaded old "nobody's going to tell me what to do" attitude that has been the downfall of my people since they got kicked out of Scotland by James VI. It's the same mindset that was our undoing during the Civil War.

"Daddy, I've really missed you," Mother said with a soft smile. "Some of the best times of my life were after Mother finally left, and you and I were keeping house together. It was hard facing people once the news got out, but at least we finally had some peace. I used to hate for her to pick me up from band practice. The car would usually stink from cigar or cigarette smoke, even though neither of you smoked. It was mortifying to know what she was doing and not be able to say anything."

Grandpa shook his head. "I knew what was going on. But I thought she'd eventually settle down. I had no idea she'd leave us for that man. You know your mother never really did have a chance to be a child. Things were so rough at her house that she got married for the first time at thirteen to get away from home. Her first husband was a widower with children almost her age. She said when they were all outside playing together she was just one of the gang, but when they went inside, she had to be the mother."

Mother's eyes widened. "She never told me any of this. Did she run out on that marriage too? Was that man Mac's father?" (My maternal grandmother had an older daughter, Bernice, before she married my grandfather.)

Grandpa shook his head again. "No, he was another man. The first husband was a veteran of World War I. He was gassed in the trenches and didn't live too long after they married. When he died, your mother was too young to support all those children. Others in the family took the kids."

"Have you had any contact with your mother since she left?"

Mother frowned, "No, I suspect she's around Houston some place, but I haven't heard from her." There was a quiet pause before Mother continued, "I'm relieved to see you're not drinking like you were for a while, Daddy, and that you're happy with your new wife. Does she know you came here today?"

Grandpa's face colored a bit, "No, she's not much older than you, and I guess she'll always be just a little insecure. You know she grew up with even less than we had."

Mother looked ready to cry. "Daddy, if you have to sneak around to visit us, it's wrong for you to be here. I'm working so hard to show these people I'm not my mother's daughter. I can't afford any problems with your wife."

He nodded and stayed a while longer. It was a great visit, but I never saw him again.

Mother loved her father and held him close to her heart. I know because she spoke of him often. My brother and sister and I have great "memories" of a grandfather we never knew, because she made him part of our lives by entertaining us with the adventures they shared. She taught us to love him.

Mother had been a junior in high school when her parents divorced, and her mother left with another man. She spoke generally of the divorce and of staying with her father to keep house for him while she finished school. She made it sound like great fun and high adventure. I would later learn their household had not been peaceful during her parents' marriage. My mother's mother and half-sister would engage in boisterous, no-holds-barred arguments that would often disintegrate into the exchange of physical blows. Grandpa McDaniel purportedly told his wife, "I have no right to dictate how you treat your child, but don't you dare beat our girl." Mother never mentioned these arguments.

My maternal grandmother had reached maturity without nurturing. She was too busy grasping for happiness and trying to fill the void in her own soul to be concerned about Mother. You have to be parented before you can be a parent.

Mother's strong attachment to her father was deeply rooted, but she was willing to sacrifice it for the love of her husband and children and to establish a "respectable" family. One of the more obvious characteristics of an abusive situation is that the victims are cut off from family and friends. Mother unwittingly helped create the isolated situation by breaking ties with the one worldly-wise person who could have been her advocate. He would have been savvy about our father's constant absence.

Fifty years later, after both my parents had died, one of our father's first cousins summarized Mother's immediate family in these terms, "Your momma and her old man were good people, but your grandma and that other girl weren't."

Greasy Staple

Breakfast on the Holcomb Place

Every kitchen in Cedar Creek had a container set between the back two burners of the kitchen range to hold bacon drippings. Some were made for that purpose with "grease" written across the front and a fine mesh strainer set just inside the top to catch the larger pieces of meat that were floating in the drippings. Mother used an old shortening can.

My parents and paternal grandparents shared a rented freezer locker in a butcher shop in Lockhart. They would have a cow and a hog butchered and the meat cut and wrapped and stored in that facility. Granny had a chest freezer at her house. Occasionally one of the men would make a run to the locker for meat and our father brought some home "on an as-needed basis."

Mother used a cast-iron skillet for frying meat. In the mornings, she would first fry bacon and then drop the eggs in the boiling bacon grease. She would tilt the skillet and use her egg turner to direct some of the grease to the top of the egg and slightly congeal the top. The results had a rough brown lacey edging I found particularly unappetizing.

Mother made biscuits on occasion, but we usually ate white bread from the general store for breakfast. We had no toaster. Toast was made by dotting the slice of bread with pieces of margarine and browning it under the oven's broiler. For a special treat, sugar and cinnamon would be sprinkled across the top.

Our father always ate two sunny-side-up eggs layered with black pepper and Tabasco sauce, and toast and bacon. Mother believed in feeding her children hot cereal in the winter. I found Cream of Wheat or oatmeal greatly preferable to eggs but still regularly lost it all on the bus ride into school, which did not place me in good standing with the driver.

If forced to eat eggs, I would demand they be scrambled. They were still totally repugnant to my taste buds, but at least, they weren't runny, and didn't remind me of the rear end of a chicken. Once or twice I tried drowning the egg in ketchup, with disastrous results. On one occasion, Joe and I were both made to remain at the breakfast table until we'd cleaned our plate. We both had scrambled eggs, but mine was the only one with ketchup. Mother left the room, and I put some of my egg on Joe's plate. I've forgotten the rest of the scenario but do recall it didn't end well for me.

There was no variety of breads to choose from at the general store. There was only one brand of plain white bread. Once in a while, Mother used some of it to make French toast. She also made pancakes occasionally. Pancakes served with the sausage made by the Lockhart butcher from a pig we had raised were my all-time favorite. I especially liked these for supper now and again.

Our father worked as a steelworker and helped to build the aluminum plant in Thorndale for a few months during the height of the drought in the mid-1950s. His lack of experience in construction was not a hindrance. All the steelworkers were farmers and ranchers desperate to make extra money during this desperate time.

Mother prepared our father's sack lunch along with breakfast each morning. She made extra toast and bacon and fried eggs for sandwiches.

Family Snapshots

This picture of my mother and paternal grandfather were taken shortly after my parents were married. Mother always claimed to be obviously pregnant with me in this shot, but I don't see it.

This is Mother seated in Granddaddy's chair on the back porch of Great-Granny Watts' house with me in her lap. She's sitting in Granddaddy Ellis's chair. It had a basket attached on the other side where he kept his magazines and cigarette papers and a can of tobacco. As a child, I thought it was huge. Note the bag hanging on the wall on the far side of the door. It held clothespins. In warm weather, this L-shaped porch was the central sitting room of the house.

This is the only picture I have of my parents with me as an infant. Notice how scrawny they were and how my father has yet to grow into his hands. This was how people looked before the advent of processed foods. As an infant, I was a caricature of my father's side of the family. Most people who lived out in the country lived in weathered, unpainted houses like the one in the background.

This snapshot of Spotty and me was taken before we moved to the Holcomb Place. I have no idea where we were living at the time but remember well how Spotty liked to take a bath in hot weather. Note the rough steps on the house in the immediate background and the sparse vegetation. The 1950's drought had obviously begun.

I believe it was our maternal grandmother's third husband who took this picture of Joe and me. It was our first Easter together on the Holcomb Place. I'm almost four; Joe, nearly one. Note the patchy vegetation on the ground and the wide treeless expanse in the background. Even though it's spring, the plant growth is sparse due to the lack of water.

I inherited a number of old photographs when my maternal grandmother died. None of them had any information on the back that would identify the subject. I do, however, have reason to believe this is my grandmother's father. He looks like a pretty stern individual, and it would be easy to understand why Grandmother would marry at 13 to escape him.

My Great-Granny Ellis is the young woman standing behind her mother in this picture. Her parents were J and Martha Smith; her brothers, Charlie and Byron. And notice how when you wear a long skirt, you don't have to keep your knees together.

Joe CHarlie
Odeen
   Maggie Lois   Elmo   J.C.   Maggie

This is my paternal great-grandparents, Joe and Maggie Ellis with their children. Great-Granddaddy is on the left with his son Charlie standing next to him. Seated in front of Charlie is Odeen. The baby seated on the hood of the car is Maggie Lois. Both my great-grandmothers on my father's side of the family had menopausal babies who spent their lives caring for elderly relatives. My paternal grandfather, J.C., is standing on the other side of the car with his brother, Elmo, seated in front of him. Grant-Granny Ellis is standing on the far right.

—CHAPTER TWO—

Pig Farming

"When my ship comes in, I'm not even going to eat bacon," our father said. He was standing at the back door covered in mud and slime with a tiny piglet cupped in his hands. His first moneymaking project on the Holcomb Place was pig farming. He had found a new litter of piglets with a runt and was bringing it to Mother for individual attention. It must have been quite a struggle to get this particular baby away from its mother.

No sow will ever win Mother-of-the Year in the animal kingdom. Sows prefer to give birth in seclusion. Once the piglets have arrived, the mother often smothers a few of the litter by napping on them. It's also common for her to develop a severe case of the "munchies" and snack on one of the more succulent newborns. Pig farming requires a basic knowledge of swine behavior patterns. No one with a delicate stomach or sensitive nose should consider the profession.

Mother found herself running a piglet clinic. Her patients were the runts, piglets with minor injuries or birth defects and those rejected by their mothers. Treatment was basic. She would swaddle each frail baby in rags and place it in a shoebox. The box was then set on the open door of the gas cook stove. The pilot light kept the baby warm. She fed the babies with an eyedropper. She had a respectable success rate, but once or twice we woke in the morning to discover Mother had misjudged how close to set the box to the pilot light. The patient was deceased and baked well done.

Screwworm infestation added an extra challenge to the project. It has since been eradicated, but was a serious problem in the 1950s. The fly would lay its eggs in any break in the skin of an animal. The gestation period for the eggs lasted as long as it takes to blink. The larvae then fed on the flesh of the host animal. The results were painful, disgusting and disfiguring, if not fatal. Some of the piglets were scarred from the infestation despite our father's vigilance.

Our two most memorable screwworm victims were born in the same litter. We named them Sadie and Snuffy Smith. Sadie was a nice enough piglet, but her brother, Snuffy, had the most pleasing personality. He had a cheerful demeanor despite the loss of one side of his nose to screwworms. Snuffy thrived under Mother's care and quickly graduated from the shoebox to larger accommodations.

An old smokehouse less than a hundred yards from our back steps became a special nursery for those animals that had outgrown Mother's makeshift intensive care unit but still required close supervision. It smelled of newborn puppies rather than smoke and cured meat.

Snuffy hung out in the back yard with the dogs once he was grown. They seemed to consider him one of the pack, despite his unfortunate mucus issue. He wasn't especially attractive, with half his nose gone, and his oink was a bit adenoidal, but his devotion to Mother endeared him to us all.

The screen on the back door was over two inches thick. It had to be reinforced with several different layers of extra heavy-duty screen to keep Snuffy from walking through it to join Mother in the house. He was her constant companion when she worked outside.

Feeding farm animals with bagged food from the feed store is expensive. Our father arranged to haul off all of an independent baker's stale baked goods. He regularly brought home a truckload of these wrapped baked goods and dumped them in the dirt-floored storage room of the barn.

These would later be unwrapped and tossed in the troughs with other feed for the pigs.

The stack of these appealing pastries was higher than my head. Their presence was frustrating to me beyond words. We were living on cornbread and pinto beans and chicken fried meat. My stomach was filled at every meal, but I craved variety.

My First Solo

Another source of hog food came from a family-style café owned by one of our father's paternal uncles in Austin. Once or twice a week our father would drive to Austin and return with a barrel or two of slop. The dishwashers swept the food the customers left on their plates into containers as part of the cleaning process. The scraps would be combined in a larger barrel our father would transport back to Cedar Creek for his hogs.

A fork or spoon was occasionally dropped into the slop. Mother disinfected these and gave them to me for digging in the dirt or for playing house. I had a collection of five or six that I kept in a shallow square box that originally contained a pair of nylon stockings.

One laundry day I decided to go exploring. Mother was distracted by caring for an infant and running back and forth between the house and washing machine with tubs of boiling water. She didn't see me leave. I wandered off up the hill along the gravel drive in the general direction of our front gate.

Spotty, my female terrier-mix, and Minnie Pearl, a tortoise-shell cat, accompanied me. Spotty had been a beloved member of our family since my second Christmas, when our father came across her and the rest of her litter abandoned along the side of the icy road. These two were my earliest childhood companions. Mother once pointed out that Minnie Pearl would stop drinking water to follow me. I now realize these two were far wiser at this point in our lives than I was. They worked hard to watch over me.

I was carrying my precious silverware in the stocking box, which slowed me down considerably. The pieces didn't fit properly in the container and kept slipping out. I'd have to stop, pick it all up, rearrange everything and then head out again.

We had ambled past the barn and stock tank and were halfway up the first hill when Mother started calling my name. I knew I wasn't lost and answered in a half-hearted manner. Mother's cries increased in frequency and urgency. I turned around and was headed back towards the house when the prized utensils fell once again. Granddaddy Ellis then came bumping down the hill in his pickup. He scooped up Spotty and me and my precious box and brought us back down the hill in less than two minutes.

Minnie Pearl was too cool to ride in a mechanical conveyance. She simply disappeared into the underbrush as the truck approached and made her way back to the house alone, in typical feline fashion.

We reached home to find Mother hysterically running around the outside of the house. She was wringing her hands and screaming my name as she ran. She burst into tears as I climbed out of the pickup. The sight of her tears made me start crying. Spotty, who was also female, began frantically barking.

Granddaddy worked hard to hide his romantic nature under a stoic façade. He was devoted to Western romances and knew the day of the month each hit which newsstand.

He couldn't bear to see a woman cry. Desperate, he said, "I'm on my way to Austin, and just stopped by to see if you need anything. If you'll all just stop crying, I'll bring back anything you want."

After a quick conference in the comfort of Mother's arms, he was sent on his way with an order for calves' liver and apricot nectar, my two most favorite things in the whole wide world.

It was after this episode that Mother decided to teach us all to be afraid of large bodies of water. She knew we would hike and explore the Holcomb property as we grew older. She didn't mind looking for us but couldn't bear the thought of dragging the stock tank as part of the search.

Whistling in the Dark

It was late summer. The sows and their offspring were due to be sent to market in the next couple of months. Mother and Joe and I quickly settled into a routine. Our father worked extremely long hours. While most farmers and ranchers were home around dark, it was not unusual for him to stay out until after 9 or 10 P.M.

On those frequent nights when we were alone, Mother would put us to bed and then sit at the kitchen table and listen to the popular programs of the day on the radio that sat on top of the refrigerator. The radio, the daily newspaper, and the five-party telephone line were her only connections to the outside world.

In warm weather, I slept on the front screened porch and could listen to the radio as I fell asleep. On this particular night, she listened to *The Snake Pit*, a play set in a mental hospital. I couldn't sleep for listening to the story. I was terrified and fascinated at the same time.

Mother switched off the radio at the end of the play. In the ensuing silence, I heard faint whistling from just beyond the barn. Mother heard it too. "Who's there?" she called.

The whistling stopped. Mother tiptoed through the house and came to sit on the edge of my bed. In a few minutes, it started again. Her second call also went unanswered. Our father arrived home an hour or so later to find Mother and me asleep together for mutual protection.

We went out of the pig business that fall. Several black men were hired to help collect the animals and prepare them for market. It was the custom of the time to provide lunch for the workers. The Caucasians were served in the house; the blacks, out under the nearest shade tree. As she handed a plate to Jake, a black man who lived in the vicinity, Mother said, "Jake, I'm happy for you to take a shortcut across our property any time you want, but I'm here alone with two children. The next time you walk whistling in front of my house in the dark, you need to answer me or I'll be forced to shoot. Do you understand?" With a sheepish grin, he accepted his plate and nodded.

Feeding the Hands

Once or twice each year, to help work his cattle our father would enlist as hired hands several of his contemporaries as well as a couple of black men, always referred to as "the hands." (I'm not sure if he paid his friends or if they worked on a reciprocity system.) To "work" cattle meant gathering the animals together and tending to their health. The men would ride out on horseback over the entire acreage to herd all the cattle into a "lot." In other parts of the West, a lot was called a corral. Gathering cattle from mesquite-covered areas was called "popping brush." A truck-driver friend of our father's once volunteered to work cattle for fun. He "popped brush" for one day and spent the next week in bed recuperating from sore muscles and wounds from the mesquite thorns embedded in his arms and legs. He hadn't worn chaps to protect his legs. Mesquite thorns are hard to dig out, and it usually takes a few days for the wound to fester enough for them to be removed.

Each animal in the lot was examined and treated as required. Most were vaccinated. A large fire was built near the lot and kept roaring to heat the irons used for branding. Our father's brand was E- (the E bar). Some of the young male animals were castrated. Calves old enough to be weaned were separated from their mothers and their ears notched to identify their ownership.

It took two or three men to hold an animal down to be branded or castrated. The work was hot and messy and loud with the squalls of terrified cattle.

On one side, most lots had a chute, a narrow passageway with a gate at either end. The exit gate had an opening through which a cow's head could be stuck and held there tightly. Horned animals were forced into the chute one at a time. The gate at the opening would be closed to confine the animal, which would then be forced to put its head through the opening. The horns would then be cut off and medication swabbed on the cut surface to prevent infection. The cattle were "dehorned" for their own protection. Some horns could grow in an arch and into the animal's head or eye. The procedure also kept them from harming each other.

A new de-horning medication was used one year. The instructions said to apply it before the horns were removed. Everyone knew the medication was highly poisonous and tried to keep track of all the horns, but obviously several were missed during the chaotic process. Our mama dog had a half-grown litter. The horns were probably missed because she took them and carefully buried them for her pups. The men could never find her hiding place. We lost several potentially valuable—not to mention dearly loved—puppies, because their mother would occasionally present a poisoned horn to one as a special treat.

Mother's responsibility during this process was to provide lunch for all the men. Pinto beans and chicken-fried steak with cream gravy and corn bread were a typical menu.

Pinto beans were served almost every day, at least once a day. Our father preferred them cooked almost to mush. It was a time-consuming process that started with picking out stones from the dried beans, which were then rinsed and soaked in water overnight. First thing the next morning, they were rinsed again and put on to cook with a large piece of pork for seasoning. Mother always bragged that she made a "mean pot of beans." The secret was in the time spent simmering and the size of the piece of pork.

Chicken-fried steak is easily prepared; it's cleaning up afterward that's difficult. Mother fried the meat in a combination of bacon fat and shortening. While this was heating up, she spread out each piece of round steak and whacked it several times with a butcher knife to tenderize it before cutting it into portion sizes. The meat would then be rolled in flour, seasoned with salt and pepper, and gingerly placed in hot grease in the cast-iron skillet.

After all the pieces were browned on both sides and had turned a dark gray in the middle, it was time to make the cream gravy. Most of the grease would be poured out of the skillet and a roux made from the seasoned flour used to coat the meat. It would always be lumpy with pieces of coating. Once it reached the desired consistency, Mother gradually added whole milk and stirred until the gravy reached the desired thickness.

The hired hands were served outside in a shady spot, while the others sat at the kitchen table. Mother was always generous with her portions. Interestingly, most of the men seated around our kitchen table swore their sensitive stomachs couldn't tolerate onions or garlic, but they smothered their food in black pepper and hot sauce.

Mother followed the community tradition and washed the hired hands' dishes after the others, not because she thought they were naturally dirty but because she feared they hadn't been vaccinated. She also added extra bleach to the water to kill any potential germs.

Mother's Cornbread

One cup corn meal
3 teaspoons baking powder
One teaspoon salt
One cup milk

3 tablespoons flour
3 teaspoons sugar
one egg

Heat approximately three tablespoons fat (bacon or shortening or combination of the two) in a 350° oven while you mix the batter. Thoroughly blend the dry ingredients. Beat the egg with the milk and then add to the dry ingredients and stir just until blended. Pour into the eight or nine inch cast iron skillet and bake until done (approximately 20 to 30 minutes).

—CHAPTER THREE—

Joe Flirts With Fire

The air at home was much sweeter once the pigs were sold. We didn't realize how much excitement they had generated until they were gone. It was really quiet on the Holcomb Place without them; quiet and lonely for Mother and Joe and me. We could spend weeks and sometimes months without going beyond our front gate, or seeing another person outside our family.

Our father continued to raise cattle and followed his usual routine. He liked to get up and away from the house before 5 A.M. There were always several nights a week when he didn't return home until around 10.

Our parents' main concern was making a living and getting ahead in the world. Child rearing was an accepted by-product of their marriage. There was never any doubt that we were loved, but children were to be seen and not heard. Our parents were more concerned with being able to feed and clothe us than whether they were using the proper parenting techniques.

Their generation had moved beyond needing a large family to help work the land, but had yet to become aware of the importance of early childhood training. Keeping house was labor-intensive. Mother spent time with us and interacted with us, but it was done as we played near where she was working. We were often sent outside to entertain ourselves while Mother tended to her indoor chores. Several instances of unintended mischief resulted from our childish curiosity and Mother's divided attention.

Joe has always been fascinated with every form of machinery and how it worked. As soon as he could walk, he began dragging things back to the house that he'd found under a bush or by the barrel where we burned our trash. Bits and pieces of toys he had disassembled to see how they worked added to the clutter.

He was also mesmerized by fire. A small butane heater with heating elements designed to look like glowing embers heated our kitchen. Mother would set a #3 galvanized wash tub in front of this to bathe us.

My brother was curious about those glowing "rocks." Bath time presented an irresistible opportunity. One evening Mother turned her back just long enough for Joe to stand up in the tub and pee into the heater. Results of the experiment were twofold: Joe confirmed to himself that the "burning rocks" were not real, while the rest of us learned how long it took a butane heater to burn away the smell of urine.

On a rare winter visit to our paternal grandparents, Granddaddy found Joe in the back bedroom playing with hot coals from the fireplace. He had used the poker and the fireplace shovel to spread a neat trail of glowing coals across the dry wooden floor.

Granddaddy had never raised his voice or laid a hand on any of us, but this was a serious offense, and he felt he had to make a serious point. A record-breaking drought had begun in the early 1950s, and there was no fire department to call for help or even a water faucet or hose to fight a fire; so he swatted Joe on the bottom a couple of times. Joe was too shocked to cry. Granddaddy, however, was distraught and had to sit and hold Joe on his lap for a while to collect his composure.

Mother appointed Joe the official trash collector and burner for our household. She would start the ceremony with the command, "Go get the wastebaskets. It's time to burn the contents." She never used the term *trash* or *garbage*. Together they took the trail down the back of the hill behind the house, where everything was burned in a barrel. She would then hand Joe one match at a time and watch him set the fire.

One afternoon Joe was especially bored and asked, "Is it time to burn contents?" They grabbed up all the refuse lying about, including a large paper bag from the kitchen floor, and were halfway down the hill with it before the cat that was napping in the bag woke up enough to protest.

Family Birthday Celebrations

Mother spent the winter Joe was three making stuffed animals and a doll bed from an apple crate for the Sunday school class in Cedar Creek. Her finest creation was a child-size Raggedy Ann doll. She finished its clothing on Granddaddy's birthday in May.

Mother baked and iced a cake in celebration of his special day. We took a bath and donned fresh clothing for the festive event. We were living in the middle of nowhere, with little variety in our lives. We had to make our own fun. Mother dressed Joe in the doll's pantaloons and dress and apron. It was an impulsive gesture intended to amuse her father-in-law.

She covered the iced cake with a tea towel and placed it on the floor of the pickup for the drive from our house to Granddaddy's, a tooth-jarring, bone-jolting four- or five-mile trip. Seat belts had yet to be invented. The cake arrived with the impression of a big toe smack dab in its center. Granddaddy smiled at the toe print, but couldn't hide his dismay at Joe's attire. That old chauvinistic Code of the West didn't include a clause for cross-dressing, not even for a toddler as a joke. Joe was darling in the costume, which only made matters worse.

Another birthday celebration resulted in a similar miscommunication regarding humor. I was five. The big social event of the year was an Ellis family reunion at Uncle Elmo's café to celebrate Granddaddy's mother's birthday. Three generations were present to be photographed with the honoree. We left through the kitchen when the party ended. The garbage cans had just been washed, and the back alley was slippery with mud. Although I was holding our father's hand, I lost my footing and splashed down on my fanny in a puddle.

Our father snatched me up and started to hit me as hard as he could with his bare hands. Granny responded with genuine amusement. One of her sisters-in-law looked out to see what was causing the commotion, and she choked out between guffaws, "Jackie Lee fell down and embarrassed her daddy."

Slimy mud ran down my leg into one sock and shoe. I hurt my tailbone in the fall and was mortified at being hit in public. "Get in the truck and stop that crying," commanded our father. I climbed in and sat in the middle, careful to leave room for him to use the gearshift. Mother held Joe in her lap. The mud gradually dried during the hour-long ride home. The pain from the fall and blows faded as my puzzlement increased over Granny's reaction to the incident. Although I didn't know the term, I sensed a sadistic quality in her sense of humor.

The next morning there was no discussion of the preceding day. Our father was gone when we woke. We were back in the routine of our quiet threesome.

Unintended Consequences

Our father had no understanding of, and little patience with, small children. If we did something that displeased him, he was quick to make his feelings known with either the flat of his hand or his wide Western belt doubled back on itself and swung full force against our bottoms and legs.

The media at the time consisted of the radio and daily newspaper. There was never any discussion on either of these that I heard regarding whether or not children should be spanked. Spanking, or at least an occasional swat on a child's posterior when warranted, was the generally accepted norm.

Psychological and emotional and verbal abuse had yet to be recognized. It is my impression that my parents' generation used the same techniques for raising their children as those that had been used to rear them. The theory was "This was the way I was treated, and I didn't turn out too bad."

Mother parented with humor and patience. She had an outrageous vocabulary and found it amusing to address a small child with big words; the more syllables, the better. Her reference to our household refuse as "contents" when talking to three-year-old Joe is a prime example.

Granny, our father's mother, had no sense of humor. She had a third-grade education and regarded anyone who made jokes as a fool. She may also have been intimidated by Mother's vocabulary. Looking back at the situation as an adult, I also suspect she resented Mother's parents. The McDaniels flaunted their time spent in honky tonks and "unrighteous" behavior, but thanks to Grandpa's steady employment enjoyed a more financially secure lifestyle while the Ellis family lived more quietly and struggled financially.

A Funeral in the Family

We received a rare long-distance phone call just before the holidays. "Ginny, Ed is dead." It was Mother's half-sister on the phone from Houston.

"Oh, Mac, I'm so sorry. What happened?" Mother asked with genuine sorrow in her voice.

"I don't know. We were getting ready to go out when he just fell across the bed and died," Mac answered.

Mother was horrified. "That's terrible. Where is he now?" she asked.

"He's right here beside me. What do I do?" She was obviously in shock. Mother had to talk her through the steps required to contact the police and call for an ambulance.

Bernice was Mother's half-sister. She had assumed her stepfather's surname and became "Mac" to her family and high school friends. Aunt Mac was six feet tall and blonde. She loved to regale us with stories of her glamorous lifestyle in Houston and was quick to laugh at Mother's poverty-stricken, barefoot-and-pregnant existence. But in a pinch, she always turned to Mother.

Granny and Granddaddy agreed to keep Joe and me for the weekend while Mother attended the funeral. It wasn't easy scraping together the funds for the round-trip bus ticket to Houston.

Mother made a point of delivering us to Granny sparkling clean. She had washed my hair and rolled it in pin curls. The next morning I asked to have my hair combed and was told it was "too much trouble." I was to leave my hair in pin curls until Mother's return. It gradually became painful. The pins that didn't fall out of their own volition gradually gouged tender places into my scalp, but it was easier to bear the comparatively minor discomfort than Granny's rage.

My paternal grandmother was the antithesis of her husband. There was no levity in her life. She managed to squeeze all the beauty and joy out of everything leaving only obligation and duty. A round-shouldered, barrel-waisted woman with pinched, judgmental lips, she wore rimless bifocals and peered down her nose at everyone. She used the bodice of her dress as a pincushion, making her literally and figuratively a prickly personality.

Also, Granny was the only woman I ever saw urinate standing up.

She harangued our father: "Who was Edward Shields to us? Why should our lives be disrupted for his funeral? If that woman is doing so well, why did you have to buy Ginny's bus ticket? You know what that woman's like. No telling how many times either she or her mother have been married, or if she was even married to this man." Seated in a deep rocking chair with his head buried in the *Austin American-Statesman*, our father merely nodded.

A Blue Norther hit over the weekend. Bitterly cold winds blew out of Canada and straight across the Midwest to Texas. Great-Granny Watts's house, where my paternal grandparents lived, had been built to endure heat rather than cold. There was little if any insulation. The windows across the front of the house were large and reached almost to the floor. The house stood off the ground a couple of feet, allowing the cold air to blow through the tiny cracks and crevices in the floor, as well as those around the windows and ill-fitting doors.

Early mornings were the most miserable. The drafty front rooms that we used the most were heated by butane heaters, but they were turned off at night. We had to sit on stools around the kitchen table and wait for the oven to heat the room as Granny made the breakfast biscuits. We were too miserable for conversation.

Granddaddy poured his coffee into a cup, added milk and sugar, stirred it a moment or two, and then poured it into a saucer to cool. Once it reached the desired temperature, he slurped it from the saucer.

Joe and I spent one of the most difficult periods of our lives closed up with Granny in three rooms that weekend. As an active toddler, there was no way Joe could avoid Granny's wrath. He endured a constant litany of threats and swats. "You look just like that weak Alva McDaniel," she would storm at him. (Alva McDaniel was our mother's father.)

Mother missed the bus home Sunday afternoon. The person who sold her the ticket, either the agent or driver, had given her the wrong time.

Granny raged when our father returned without Mother. She cornered me in the kitchen, "You know your mother's a no-good fool, don't you? Well, don't you?" She had me by the shoulders and bent down until we were almost nose-to-nose and shook me slightly with every "don't you?" I finally nodded and mumbled agreement just to make her stop. I then slipped away from the kitchen to the bathroom at the far end of the house as quickly as I dared.

There I closed the door and leaned against it for a moment to collect my thoughts. It was an unheated, makeshift room. All the surfaces of the room were of bead board and painted battleship gray. The tub emptied straight down on the ground beneath the floor. There was no water connection to the toilet. A bucket stood nearby was used to fill the toilet tank to flush it.

Hair had escaped the pin curls and fallen into my face

at odd angles. I pushed it away in misery, knowing I had just betrayed the one person in the world who loved me the most. A heavy lump of guilt and shame gathered in my chest and has never quite gone away.

The Christmas Boots

It was always a huge relief to get back home with Mother after an extended period in Granny's company. This was especially true around the holidays. Mother made it a magical time, one of the best. Santa brought Joe and me matching red cowboy boots. I was convinced they carried super powers.

It rained just enough after the holidays to turn the clay front of the house into red mud. On the first laundry day of the New Year, while Mother was busy, I led Joe to the ditch to test those powers by walking across the mud. We sank to the tops of our boots by the third step. Joe was firmly stuck and simply stood there. It was up to me to get us out of the mess I had instigated. I pulled my feet out of my boots and walked back to the house in my stocking feet.

Mother was immediately suspicious, "Where's Joe?" she asked.

In a futile attempt to be off-hand, I answered, "Joe who?"

I was not punished for leading an expedition through mud. I wish I had been. A quick swat would have been less painful and quicker than the lecture I endured while Mother retrieved Joe and our boots. They were never quite the same after that adventure.

We wore our boots all winter and through the spring until the weather warmed up enough for us to go barefoot. Mother baked a pie for Easter and put it under the broiler to brown the top. She was hunkered down in front of the oven to make sure it didn't get too brown, when she was struck on the head from behind. Joe hit her over the head with one of his boots. She literally saw stars. When she could focus again, he was sitting at the kitchen table and beating time with the same boot as he sang, "Jesus Loves Me."

This was one of Mother's favorite "Joe stories." She said he looked so angelic singing the hymn that it was obvious he didn't realize how much he had hurt her.

Joe's boots were bronzed when he outgrew them. Mine were simply discarded, but my reputation was pretty well set.

—CHAPTER FOUR—

The Past Shapes the Future

A family is a loosely organized group of astonishingly hurtful people related by blood or marriage. Influence from earlier ancestors may be diluted with time, but it never completely fades. It's as though we all live in a huge body of water, and each of us is a stone. The people who lived generations before us may be dead, but the ripples they caused with their personalities and behavior are still in motion. It was Faulkner who said, in *Requiem for a Nun*, "The past is never dead. It's not even past."

Both sides of my family had similar humble Scots-Irish origins. Neither had ever known anything but poverty. Many had volatile tempers. Some were prone to violent outbursts. They were ashamed of their shortcomings, real and imagined. Pride forced them to be secretive to conceal their flaws.

Mother's family, the McDaniels and Franklins, had a broad sense of humor and outstanding verbal skills. Our father's family, the Ellis/Watts side did not. The McDaniel women hung out in bars, while the Ellises were straight-laced. Most of the Ellis men pretended to follow their wives' examples but quietly strayed when the opportunity presented itself. Sometimes they created the opportunity.

The only Watts who openly drank was a maternal uncle

of my father who was a binge alcoholic. He was also a chain-smoker and drove a gasoline tanker truck.

The Ellis/Watts family had a vague sense of their history. Hazy references were frequently made to one great-grandmother who had migrated from Kentucky to Texas. No exact details were ever given. A reference to her name at a family gathering would be met with an exchange of rueful grins among those who had known her.

Mother's side of the house didn't share any family stories beyond their own experiences. Her mother did have siblings, but we never met any of them. Grandmother had a number of brothers and sisters. One brother was aptly named Jesse James Franklin. Mother described him as a germaphobic petty criminal. We never had enough time with Grandpa McDaniel for him to expound on his ancestry.

Shame generated by poverty kept both sides of the house from sharing stories of deceased relatives with their children. Mother knew one of her grandfathers died when he had a stroke in front of the fireplace. He was a big, tall man, and fell face first into the fire. His petite wife managed to pull him out and nursed him for some time before he finally succumbed to the combination of the stroke and serious burns. It's too bad their names are lost. Like countless others, they labored hard and suffered greatly to settle this country.

In the early 20th century, two deaths in the Ellis/Watts family influenced the following generations. The first was J.C. Ellis, Jr., our father's elder brother. He died of a brain tumor at thirteen. When the symptoms began, Granny and Granddaddy Ellis owned a general store in Garfield, a small community that's now a suburb of Austin. Their means were severely limited, as was relevant medical knowledge.

As adults, my brother and sister and I have discussed this period and decided it was probably pivotal in the development of our father's personality. He was undoubtedly exposed to his brother's suffering and then sent to live for an extended period with his maternal grandparents, where he may have spent most of his time in the company of his grandfather, Perry Watts. He was 12 years old. It must have been horrific for him. If he witnessed any of his brother's suffering, it probably scared him terribly. His parents may have been too grief-stricken over the loss of one child to give much emotional support to the other.

Our father grew up to be a cattle dealer and was respected for his knowledge of livestock. He may have absorbed this knowledge from his grandfather during Junior's illness. We do know he suffered a minor injury while helping his grandfather with some hogs. He got too close to an old boar hog that cut his knee with a glancing blow of its tusk. It left a permanent gaping hole in one of his knees.

Granny Ellis never discussed her personal feelings with me. She made only one allusion to Junior and his illness in my presence. She said the doctors asked to perform an autopsy after he died. She refused. She said he had "been through enough." I gather from this understatement that it had been a long and painful illness. It must have been hell on earth to sit and watch your child suffer and be powerless to do anything about it.

Granny was so mean and angry and critical it was hard to be sympathetic. Once in a great while, Mother would be forced to leave us in Granny's care. With adult retrospect, I believe Granny was angry over my parents' marriage. She never thought Mother was good enough for our father, but the Virgin Mary herself probably wouldn't have fared much better. Joe was an easy target. She viewed his sweet and gentle nature as being "weak," and never missed an opportunity to swat him or to verbally berate him. Her attitude towards him was condescending and demanding.

A booklet entitled *The Art of Suffering* was prominently displayed on the desk in the entry hall of her house. We children couldn't understand how anyone who caused such misery could actually be in pain and laughed among ourselves about it.

Junior died in June of 1935. In 1944, our father's grandfather, William Perry Watts, Sr., died. Throughout my childhood my family spoke of him as though they expected him to walk in the back door at any moment. Today I could take you to the exact spot where he turned his first car over in a ditch.

It was his mother who brought him from Kentucky to Texas. Family legend has it that her husband deserted her, and she moved to get a fresh start. Great-Granddaddy Watts was kicked in the face by a mule or horse during the journey. This incident is a particular puzzle to the current family, since they were said to have made the journey by train. But one way or another, his jaw was severely injured, forcing his mother to leave him with a doctor in a small town in Louisiana. After months of struggling to repair the damaged jaw, the doctor was forced to remove the lower jawbone and attached teeth.

Great-Granddaddy grew a beard to cover the loose flap of skin that had once covered his chin. He grew up to become a cattle dealer. In his early thirties, he charmed sixteen-year-old Jessie Alexander into eloping with him.

The marriage between W.P. Watts and Jessie Alexander produced six children: three girls and three boys. My paternal grandmother was Zula, his second daughter. The first two girls grew up to be judgmental and critical women while their mother was known throughout the area as the soul of gentle kindness. What happened in the family to produce this disparity is one of its biggest mysteries. The family can only speculate about this and wonder if there was some co-relation between their behavior as adult women and the blow to the head their father received as a youngster. Or could it have been that the parents were partial to the boys? We'll never know.

Granny and Granddaddy Ellis lost the general store sometime after the death of their son. Granddaddy was a saintly man, but saints aren't usually good businessmen. Mother once alluded to a promissory note Granddaddy signed for a friend. The friend reneged and Granddaddy wound up paying the bank. He worked a number of jobs in an effort to support his family, but they never had a secure income. Granddaddy also sustained an eye injury from flying gravel while working as a truck driver.

The facts are also fuzzy about when my grandparents moved in with my paternal grandmother's parents. One explanation is that Great-Granddaddy Watts developed heart trouble and needed help running his spread. The other version is that they moved there after Great-Granddaddy Watts died. In either scenario, the children met without their mother's knowledge and decided on her living arrangements.

Great-Granny Watts was sixty when her husband died. Sixty was considered old back then. She didn't drive and lived in a remote area. The children decided she shouldn't live alone. The land and livestock her husband left were her only source of income. It was determined that my Granny and Granddaddy Ellis would move in with her. Granddaddy leased her land and raised cattle. This provided them both with a less than modest income.

The flaw in this plan was that Granny Ellis despised Great-Granny Watts and took no pains to hide it. Great-Granny handled this toxic situation by packing her bags and spending six weeks with each of her children and her youngest brother, Lee Alexander. She followed this circuit until she died in her mid-80s.

The Dawn of Reality

I recall a warm spring day when Granny drove Mother to a doctor's appointment. Joe and I were left with Granddaddy. Joe was almost four, and I was nearly six. We were trying extra hard to be good. Granddaddy had promised us Coke floats "after a while."

He always kept his horse, Dusty, saddled during the day and tethered at the tree by the dining- room window. He put both of us up in the saddle and led us around the 20 or so acres that made up the back yard. It was heady stuff to be allowed the privilege of riding Dusty and having Granddaddy all to ourselves. He was one of the few adults we knew who would converse with small children.

Granddaddy and Dusty were a study in stoic patience. Granddaddy ambled leisurely along over the rocky ground in his high-heeled boots, the reins loosely gripped in one hand. His answers to my childish chatter were absent-minded. Dusty plodded along behind Granddaddy. A small puff of dust rose with every jolting step she took. She walked with her head down, ignoring Joe's frequent nudges in her ribs and his cries of "Yeee Haaa."

After our ride was over, Granddaddy was leading us back to tether Dusty when a voice called out, "Y'all make a happy picture." It was Mr. Barnett. He was standing on the outside of the gate of to the drive that led to the outbuildings back of the house. His hat was on the back of his head, and he was leaning on the top rail and smiling across the expanse of the drive at us.

Mr. Barnett was a minor celebrity in our household because he was Granddaddy's best friend. He was also the independent baker who sold his stale pastries to our father to feed his hogs. Granddaddy tethered Dusty to the tree. He said, "You children can go play in the blacksmith shop if you want."

Joe bounced across the gravel drive to climb on the anvil. I hung back with the men. Fido and Butchie, Granddaddy's dogs, were resting in the shade of the tree. Earlier that afternoon I had tried to pet them and would have been mauled if Granddaddy hadn't intervened.

I clearly recall the two men leaning on either side of the weathered gate and Granddaddy remarking, "This is pretty much all I'm good for anymore."

The remark jolted me. It made me really look at him. His face was etched in grief with deep lines about the eyes and his down-turned mouth. I realized the movements I had seen as leisurely were actually forced. His posture was that of a man bent with weariness and defeat. It made me want to weep. I had yet to learn about depression. That would come over the years.

Joy Beth

Mother went to the doctor that day to confirm her third pregnancy. At Easter dinner the extended family gathered around the table at Great-Granny Watts's house. Granny's older sister glared at Mother and demanded, "Why are you having another? You can't take care of the children you already have." This outspoken, hurtful behavior was typical of

Granny and her elder sister, Sallie. Although none of "my people" will ever be eligible for the diplomatic corps, I can understand how Aunt Sallie must have felt. She didn't have any children. It must have hurt terribly to see an in-law with severely limited means easily conceive and bear children.

I had heard fragments of conversation regarding Aunt Sallie's husband, Uncle Carl. I caught the word "impotent" but didn't understand it or the snickers when someone remarked that Aunt Sallie's judgmental glare was enough to take the starch out of any man.

Mother and Joe and I spent most of that summer totally alone in the log cabin on the Holcomb Place. It had originally been one square room of hand-hewn logs. A kitchen and rail-less porch had been added at the back. A screened porch covered the front, and a bedroom had been added at the end of the front porch. In the corner of the porch where the bedroom had been added to the house, the intersection of the logs and the mud used to fill in the spaces between them were still visible.

The main room was heated by a fireplace. The floor of the fireplace was a rock almost as large as the room and about three feet tall. The house was built on stilts of logs and logs combined with boulders to hold it above the rock. A level had obviously been missing from the original builders' toolbox.

A man-sized section of the wall to the left of the fireplace would open with difficulty. Stairs behind it led to a sleeping loft. I lived in this house for over ten years and never dared explore the upstairs. The incident of the snake falling out of the ceiling in our earlier residence when I was an infant had totally traumatized Mother. She and I were alone at home when, without any warning, a snake simply fell through one of the holes in the ceiling and landed on the floor in the middle of the room. Mother slept for years with a flashlight on the floor on her side of the bed. She habitually woke once or twice every night to shine the flashlight on me to be sure there wasn't an uninvited wild animal sharing my bed. That one incident convinced her that the attic of every log cabin was snake-infested.

The house was wired for electricity. A single bulb hung from the middle of the ceiling in the kitchen and main room. The walls had been covered with sheetrock. The kitchen was papered in a large floral print. The main room was painted two shades of blue, a job begun by Mother who mixed the paint and painted half the room before she caught a virus and had to go to bed. Our father mixed the second can of paint with slightly different proportions of white to blue and finished the job. There was no money for another can of paint. The main wall of the central room was evenly divided into two shades of blue the entire time we lived there. The floors were covered in nondescript, extensively cracked brown linoleum. Once in a while, when we pushed a toy across the floor, a square nail, black and unevenly shaped and probably handmade, would appear from under it.

The newspaper came in the mail six days a week. Otherwise, our only contact with the outside world was the radio that stood on top of the refrigerator in the kitchen. Mother played it most of the day for company.

We had a telephone, but it was a party line we shared with Granny and three other families. Granny listened in on Mother's conversations. Our father habitually stopped by his mother's every afternoon. During these visits, Granny would criticize Mother's conversations and phone habits to him until Mother stopped using the phone except for pressing business or emergencies.

The doctor who was attending Mother during this pregnancy was in Austin. In the late stage of the pregnancy, she phoned him. She must have been seriously concerned. It was a long-distance call. "Doctor, there's something just not right about this pregnancy," she said.

"Well, sweetheart," was his reply, "just get your boyfriend to bring you in, and I'll check you out." Mother was furious and embarrassed. She was afraid Granny might have been listening to that conversation and cause a ruckus in the family, so she simply kept her concerns to herself and let the matter drop.

Due to our isolation, our pets played a deeply significant role in our lives, maybe a greater one than most pets usually do. They were our companions, so when one went missing, it left a void. Our cat, Minnie Pearl, disappeared that summer. Without bringing it to our attention, Mother searched the brush and fields and woods around the house until she finally found the body. Minnie had been bitten by a rattlesnake. But another anonymous cat had a litter that kept us entertained most of the summer. Spotty got into the act and tried a hand at nursing the kittens, displaying such a strong nurturing instinct that I wondered if she'd been neutered too early.

Grandmother Miller

Joe and I were playing with the new kittens in the dust under the house one afternoon while Mother stood in the room just over our heads, ironing. A sedan pulled up to the back porch. I heard Mother put down the iron. She walked barefoot out to greet the unexpected company at the back door.

It was my maternal grandmother. Her new husband was with her. He was not the man she'd been with when she left her family several years earlier. Grandmother took pains to photograph Mother barefoot and pregnant. She also took pictures of Joe and me, with our dirty bare feet and our threadbare play clothes. She would take these back to Houston, where she and Bernice would laugh at Mother's poverty. The two were quick to poke fun at Mother and equally quick to turn to her in time of trouble or sorrow. Mother knew what they were doing but loved them nonetheless: They were family.

Ed Miller was Grandmother's latest husband. He won our hearts on the first visit when he brought Joe a bucket of nails. Granddaddy Ed worked for the Duncan Coffee Company. The only white-collar worker in our family, he knew exactly how to please little boys. While an addition was built on to the coffee company, he spent considerable time picking up for Joe nails the workmen had dropped. This kept Joe entertained and in mischief the rest of the summer. The first thing he built was a trap door to the back of the old smoke-house for the dogs to use.

It was after supper on one of the rare evenings our father joined us for a meal. I was playing in the back of his pickup when he came out to retrieve something from the glove compartment. The next thing I knew, he had me by one upper arm and yanked me out of the bed of the truck in one quick movement. He started pulling off his belt before I had both feet on the ground. He doubled it and proceeded to flail at my bare legs and bottom. I danced around to avoid the blows, but he continued to hold on to my upper arm. When he finished, my legs bore bloody stripes.

These furious beatings always took place in the privacy of our home. No one outside our immediate family ever witnessed one. When he started lashing out at one of us children, Spotty would put herself in the middle and bark at the top of her voice. Mother always came and watched, but never said a word. It's interesting to consider in retrospect. Father never kicked the dog. Mother always maintained a neutral attitude during one of these episodes, but the instant it was over, she would clean all of us up and put us to bed. I realize now that was her method of getting us out of the way until our father's temper cooled.

When he went out to his truck that evening, our father saw there was a nail hammered into his spare tire. He punished me because I was the child nearest at hand.

There was always an air of uncertainty tinged with dread in our household because we never knew when he would erupt. The sudden beatings made me feel sick and vacant inside. I was eager to not be hit again, and puzzled about why he would lash out at me when I was obviously not the guilty party.

It was about this time that Mother suggested we start addressing our father as "Papa." She thought it sounded more affectionate. Mother constantly praised our father to us and built him up in our eyes as a larger-than-life figure. She taught us to adore the man, despite his behavior. Our father reveled in his position in the family and was fond of pointing out, "I'm the daddy here, and you'll always do what I tell you whether it makes sense to you or not."

There are several plausible explanations for his behavior. Violent tempers did run in Great-Granny Watts' family. One of the more popular stories handed down from that branch features one of her first cousins, renowned for his quick and violent temper. According to the story, the fiery-tempered young man threw himself off the back of a wagon and into the middle of the road, where he proceeded to writhe about in fury. A female cousin watched the performance and then told him, "One of these days, you're going to pitch a fit like that, and wind up in the mental hospital." Fifty years later, that's exactly what happened. The same female cousin visited him and he begged her, "You know I'm not crazy. Please get me out of here." Her response: "You got yourself in here. Now figure out how to get yourself out." Our father may have inherited this same temper.

Our father's mother always referred to him as "the Baby" and never refused him anything. She spoiled him. Undoubtedly, this was a direct result of losing her eldest son to a sudden, mysterious illness.

His mother also did everything possible to undermine our parents' marriage. It was obvious that our father loved Mother, but I also suspect he felt tied down and resented it. His furious lashing out at the most available small child was an obvious gesture of frustration. He was caught between the two women he loved most.

There was also the aggravation of trying to establish a career in agriculture during the early days of a record-breaking drought.

Mother had another girl in December and named her Joy Beth for her two favorite Christmas carols. She had been correct about something not being right about the pregnancy: the baby was breech-born and tried to back into this world.

Ironing

There were no synthetic fabrics or steam irons in the 1950s. Most of our clothing was 100% cotton. The rumpled look was regarded as slovenly rather than hip. An extra step on wash day was devoted to all the clothing that required ironing. Once the clothing was rinsed, it was then dipped in another tub containing a solution of water and starch. Starch was sold in powdered form that came in a box from the grocery. Stiffness of the clothing was controlled by the ratio of starch to water.

When the starched pieces came off the clothesline, Mother straightened each piece one at a time on the kitchen table, one on top of another. She then sprinkled water over each piece and rolled it in a tight bundle. Some women kept a soda bottle with a unique stopper in it especially for this chore. The stopper had holes in it to finely sprinkle water as the bottle was shaken. Once all the pieces were sprinkled and tightly folded, they would all be wrapped in either a large towel or a tablecloth and stuck in the bottom of the refrigerator, at least overnight. This gave the moisture time to become more evenly distributed throughout.

It would take Mother at least one full day to do all the ironing. In the winter, I'm sure it was a more pleasant chore than most to stand over the warm iron, but on the other hand, it had to be pure misery to tackle the same job in summer under a tin roof in a room with little ventilation.

According to Mother, raisins were one of my favorite foods as a toddler and habitually tucked one or two in the pocket of my pinafore. What's the fun of having a pocket, if you don't use it? She tried to remember to always check my pinafores before ironing but once in a while she'd run an extremely hot iron across the front of a pinafore with a resulting sizzle that announced the presence of a raisin she'd missed. There was nothing to do but put that smock back in the dirty clothes to be rewashed.

Connecting Names and Faces

When I decided to include family pictures in *Raiders and Horse Thieves*, I took my collection of old family photographs to a photography lab to have them copied. Several photographers were lounging about with the proprietor and were immediately taken with my family treasures.

They poured over my photographic antiques discussing

the techniques and cameras and film and exposure used. They spoke respectfully of the results these earlier photographers had achieved with such rudimentary equipment. The photographers viewed my tattered family snapshots as examples of pioneer photography, while I treasured them as images of beloved family. They can also be studied as commentary on the socioeconomic status of the subjects and the social values of the time.

Shown below are my father's parents, Zula Watts Ellis and J.C. Ellis. These studio pictures are an unusual size designed specifically for my father to carry in his wallet during World War II. He obviously was acutely aware of being away from Texas for the first time, because he specifically requested that Granddaddy wear his Stetson. It was an easy way to display his Texas pride.

This is my maternal grandmother, Rose Franklin Miller.

There are obvious contrasts between my grandmothers that can be seen in their photographs. Grandmother Miller is dressed in a younger, more sophisticated style than Granny Ellis. She's wearing makeup, and Granny isn't. Granny Ellis was always part of a family dependent upon agriculture and without a regular income, while Grandmother either held a salaried position or was married to someone who was.

Grandmother appears comfortable in front of the camera, as though accustomed to being photographed, while Granny looks stiffly posed and serious. I know that look; without too much provocation she could burst into tears. Both Ellis grandparents are wearing expressions of mixed emotions; easily understandable. They lost their eldest son to an inexplicable illness and are presenting a brave front as they prepare to send their last son out to fight in World War

II. He's enlisted for the duration of the war. They are proud of him for doing his duty to his country, but once he's gone, they have no idea when or if they will ever see him again. They know what it is to lose a child and are terrified it may happen again.

This is Alva McDaniel, my mother's father. This man is obviously not involved in agriculture. At the time this was taken, he was working as a mechanic for Humble, a precursor to Exxon. His regular paycheck placed him in a more stable financial situation than my Ellis grandparents. Notice the cigar he's holding. Granddaddy Ellis rolled his own cigarettes. He's standing in front of a painted house with landscaping around the foundation which indicates a certain level of financial security. Mother's family lived in a neighborhood that was built and owned by Humble. Bastrop natives called it the Humble Camp.

My grandfathers did share one major personality characteristic: They were both loving and kind to their children and grandchildren. Grandpa McDaniel lied to the Social Security Division and subtracted five years from his age to keep working and support the second family he sired after he divorced my mother's mother. It could be argued that both were more "maternal" and nurturing than their wives.

Treasured Photographs

I've included the following because they're some of my favorites, and because I think they're interesting from socio-economic and historical perspectives as well.

The stamp-size original of this photograph spent decades either caught in a crevice on a closet shelf or between other items stored there, and fell out when Granddaddy's sister-in-law decided to do some spring cleaning. It was so tiny we're lucky she saw it fall. At the time it was taken, photographs must have been terribly expensive, and the stamp size was the most they could afford to share with family.

This picture of J.C. Ellis, Jr. was taken about 1922. His elaborate clothing and confident facial expression are those of a cherished child who knows his family loves him. It took skill to crochet the fancy hat he's wearing. The great pains that were taken in his attire are a reflection of the regard his family had for him.

Photography was in a relatively early stage of development in the 1930s. Cameras were too expensive, and the developing process too complex for individual ownership. It was a custom of the time for photographers to go door to door and take snapshots of the neighborhood children. The photographers also provided props for the children to pose. It made the experience fun for the child rather than a chore and produced a happy, relaxed picture.

The picture above could have been taken as early as 1927 or '28. This is J.C. Ellis, Jr, posed on the photographer's Shetland pony. The hat, bandana and chaps were also part of the packaged deal. It didn't matter that the hat is a trifle too large. Junior inherited the family ears, and they're propping it up.

The windows behind Junior reflect a nearby house, indicating that the family resided in a community, rather than out in the remote countryside. There's no landscaping around the foundation. This represents a family in a modest situation, but they were affluent enough to paint the house and have the children's picture taken.

This is Harry Gordon Ellis, my father. This was probably taken around 1930. They must have made an appointment for it, because this is obviously not a spontaneous snapshot. The subject is scrubbed until he almost glows; his hair is still wet and sharply parted. He's also dressed in his Sunday best. The goat is well trained, and takes the ideal stance to show off the elaborately painted wagon to its best advantage. Note the painstakingly painted wheels and how they're posed for the picture.

This appears to be the same house. The picture must have been taken in the unpaved driveway. The ruts in the ground indicate recent rain, and the side of the house is dirty from being splashed.

My father is the short boy on the right end. He's standing by his older brother, Junior. The third boy from the right is Perry Watts, Jr., the youngest child of Great-Granny Watts. Although he's nearly the same

age as the other children, Perry, Jr. belongs to the preceding generation. He was our father's playmate as well as his uncle. The other children are cousins from the Watts side of the family.

Their attire is typical for children of that particular time and
place. They are obviously not accustomed to being photographed.

This family studio portrait of my parents with Joe and me was used for
a Christmas card in 1951. I'm about five and Joe nearly two. Joe has a
crooked grin like my father's brother.

—CHAPTER FIVE—

Fowl Business

Our parents began to prepare for their first turkey crop during the final months of Mother's third pregnancy. They spent weeks repairing the turkey houses and roosts and pens. Turkeys are delicate. The situation may have changed, but in the 1950s, they were highly susceptible to coccidiosis, a disease thought to be carried by chickens.

The first order of business was to sell the few chickens we owned, including my bantam rooster. Chickens are pretty far down on the cuddly-pet scale, but this little guy had such a big attitude, I couldn't help but love him. He refused to stay with the other bantams and hung out with the regular-sized chickens instead. It was funny to watch him strut among the hens. His self-image was obviously inflated. He had delusions of adequacy and considered himself cock of the walk and lord of the henhouse. The hens looked down their beaks at him, but he was oblivious.

"We're going to have to sell your rooster," our father announced. Before I could draw breath to protest, he added, "and you can have the money from his sale." Reality had yet to dawn on me. I assumed my rooster was headed to a different barnyard where he might be appreciated by a new flock. I didn't understand it meant the arrogant little bird was headed straight to a cooking pot.

I watched them collect the poultry and load them for market with dollar signs running through my head. My day was spent in delightful anticipation of the huge sum I knew was headed my way.

Our father was surprised to find me waiting up for him when he returned late that night. "How much did my rooster bring?" I asked before he could close the back door. He handed me two quarters. "Fifty cents?" I was outraged. "That was a fine bantam rooster. He was worth way more than fifty cents. Do you have the bill of sale?"

My parents shared an amused glance. Our father went back out to the pickup, rummaged in the glove compartment, and returned with a rumpled itemized list of the birds sold. At the very bottom, almost as an afterthought, was listed one bantam rooster, $0.50.

I retired for the night in disgust. What was the world coming to when such a personable rooster went unappreciated?

Our father and two hired men, Duval and Jesse, were working on the big poultry house in preparation for the turkeys. The building hadn't been used for a number of years and required major repairs. Large brooders had to be installed to keep the chicks warm when they first arrived. Screens had to be replaced in the big windows that took up more than half of the two main walls. The entire building had to be secured in defense against the usual predators, including raccoons, foxes and bobcats. Once they completed this renovation, there was a smaller poultry building that required similar attention.

Beware the Hitchhiker

With the men working at home, we were able to take the pickup to church and Sunday school a little more regularly than usual. Our attendance there had been an iffy matter up to this point. Our father would rise as usual on Sunday morning. He would promise as he left that if he didn't find too much to do that morning out in the pasture, he would return in time for us to take the truck to church. We would dress in anticipation of the outing. At least a third of the time, he wouldn't return. Mother would then have to change us back into our play clothes and give us the usual pep talk about how hard our father worked and how important it was to the family that we make these small sacrifices.

Church attendance was a challenge. Dressing three small children and making the arduous drive into Cedar Creek was a daunting task. A shoe or other integral piece of apparel was always misplaced, not to appear until the last possible moment. I learned to always look under the refrigerator for missing shoes.

Joy was such a good baby we almost left her at home the first time we went to church after she was born. Mother and Joe and I beat our usual frantic path through the pets to the pickup. We sat there a moment and then Mother said, "This isn't right. What have we forgotten?" It was the baby who was happily waving her hands in the middle of our parents' bed.

It was a struggle for Mother to dress appropriately on our limited budget. The only makeup she wore was lipstick and then only to church or other public functions. When the contents of the tube were used down to a few grains in the bottom crevices, she would use a toothpick to scrape it out. She never had more than one pair of nylons.

It took practice and subterfuge to get us all into the truck and keep our pets away from us in the process. There were a number of dogs in the backyard who expected to be petted or wanted to rub up against one of us the moment the back door opened. These were to be avoided at all costs, to keep us clean and Mother's nylons unsnagged.

This had been a particular challenge back when Snuffy Smith, our pet pig, was hanging out with the dogs. It wasn't considered appropriate to show up for services reeking of Eau de Swine. We also had to keep a sharp eye on Spotty, my terrier-mix dog, who loved to climb onto the running board after we were in the truck to hitch a ride with us. The road was so rough we couldn't understand how she managed to not fall off and get run over by the back wheels.

Mother didn't have a driver's license and only drove locally. She used the white-knuckle approach. The truck was of pre-World War II vintage. It shimmied and bumped its way through the gravel and ruts of our drive. Joe stood up on the bench seat of the truck slightly behind Mother's right shoulder. She hoped to be able to brace him if necessary.

There was a gate at the end of our drive. Passing through it with a carload of children was a complicated process. Mother had to stop the truck and turn off the motor for safety's sake. She would then get out and open the gate. She had to push the gate all the way open and anchor it some way to keep it from closing on the truck as she drove through. She then walked back to the truck, started it, drove through the gate, and turned off the motor again. She would get out of the truck a second time, walk back to close the gate, return to the truck, restart the motor and drive on to church.

Driving on gravel could be like maneuvering on ice. The tires had a tendency to slip on the rocks. The lane was only wide enough to accommodate one vehicle at a time. Although the County Road Commissioner regularly had the ruts bulldozed smooth and spread with fresh gravel, they quickly returned in the most frequently traveled areas, and the fresh gravel was thrown to the sides. The curves were especially treacherous.

Down the hill and around the second curve, we crossed the rattling bridge with its canopy of rusty iron. The homey sound of the boards knocking together as the truck crossed was a sharp contrast to the view beneath the bridge. Below was a dark foreboding place with a few scummy puddles surrounded by thick underbrush. No one ever ventured down there. It wasn't the fear of encountering rattlesnakes or trolls that kept us away: it was the chiggers.

Just a few hundred yards beyond the bridge, the lane ended in a T at the Farm-to-Market Road. We turned right. Mother gripped the steering wheel at the ten and two position, cranked the speedometer up to 35 m.p.h. and launched into a lusty version of "Jesus Loves Me" to get us into the proper frame of mind.

One morning we saw a hitchhiker up ahead on our side of the road. "Quick!" Mother commanded. "Roll up your window." She wanted to make sure no stranger would be able to step up on the running board, grab hold of the door handle, open the door, and snatch one of her children as the truck shook, shimmied, and vibrated past.

In fifteen minutes or so, we passed the Cedar Creek city limit sign, which stated the population: I've forgotten the exact figure, but do remember it was a little over 300. The sign intrigued me during my early grammar-school years. I tried counting the houses in Cedar Creek from the vantage point of the school bus, and could never find more than thirteen to fifteen. How could over three hundred people fit into that little space?

We turned left at Ms. Sophie Smith's two-story house, which was said to have once been an inn for stagecoach passengers. The simple white church building with its tall steeple was about two blocks ahead on the left. We pulled into its empty parking lot. Mother looked at me in panic. "It is Sunday, isn't it?" she asked. We had never been the first to arrive. We sat a moment in quiet astonishment before another family or two rolled into the parking lot to join us.

Keeping the Sabbath

There was only one church for Caucasians in Cedar Creek. The building was shared by the Baptists and Methodists. Both denominations considered it a mission church and alternated Sundays sending out young student ministers to practice their preaching. The congregation averaged less than a dozen on most Sundays.

The church was basic. The double front doors opened directly into the sanctuary. Windows flanking the sides were whitewashed. A deep red carpet runner ran up the aisle and covered the altar. Matching red draperies hung behind the altar to cover a set of double windows and adjust the acoustics. It was probably less expensive to hide the windows under fabric than to remove them. A battered upright piano, almost in tune, stood to the right of the altar.

Classrooms for Sunday school were added to the church in a second phase of construction.

The focal point of the sanctuary was a framed print of Jesus Christ that hung in the middle of the draperies. He was depicted as an angelic, clean-shaven, fair-skinned figure with perfectly coiffed shoulder-length reddish-brown hair. His robes were immaculate. A huge halo surrounded his head.

The image always bothered me. It didn't match the Biblical stories about the Messiah with fire in his eyes who roamed the desert for forty days and nights eating locusts. This man was too clean and mild and pale. The Christ I studied lost his temper and ran the moneylenders out of the temple. I gradually came to realize this was the Scots-Irish version of the Messiah. A historically correct depiction of Christ would have shown an unkempt, swarthy man, almost Negroid in appearance; but who, in the Jim Crow era of the 1950s, would not have been comforting to the congregation.

Ms. Edith Champion was the usual pianist at church. She was a tolerant soul who bore Great-Great-Uncle Lee's unmerciful teasing with a strained grace. Great-Great-Uncle Lee (Great-Granny Watts's baby brother) was one of the few men who regularly attended church. He was also one of only two men in our family, Granddaddy being the other, who was as tolerant of little girls as he was of little boys.

He married Julia Hendrix, a schoolteacher, later in life. They had no children of their own. The fact that Aunt Julia developed a migraine every time Great-Great-Uncle Lee slept in the same room with her may have been a factor. Great-Great-Uncle Lee and Aunt Julia spent their leisure volunteering for the community. They were either related to, or long-time friends with, everyone else, and managed to nurture most of the citizenry regardless of race or social standing.

Great-Great-Uncle Lee passed the collection plate at church and counted the money as it was dropped in the plate. If he didn't think the contribution was adequate, he would simply continue to stand in the same spot wearing a gentle smile and occasionally shaking the plate until the mortified congregant added more to the plate. Ms. Champion, who sat in front at the piano, was his favorite target.

The sermons were usually uninspiring. The minister was always mindful that he was preaching to two different denominations. We usually got a double helping of "Jesus loves us" and "suffer the little children come unto Me."

Sunday afternoons were my least favorite time of the week. The Sunday paper with the color comics was delivered with Saturday's mail, leaving us with nothing new to look at or try to read. The radio only offered ball games. Sunday afternoons seemed to last a week.

This is the church in downtown Cedar Creek. In the 1950s, it was one of the few painted buildings there. Note the tin steeple.

—CHAPTER SIX—

Turkey Bonding

Joy was nine months old. It was September 1951, in central Texas. The baby had a runny nose for a couple of days. Fall weather is always a strong contrast of hot days and chilly nights. We assumed the extreme changes in temperature caused her sniffles.

That month 1,500 turkey chicks were delivered to the Holcomb Place. This was Mother's second turkey crop. They came crammed like giant pizzas in huge square boxes. Mother spent one entire day kneeling on the floor of the poultry house working with these babies. She took each one individually from the box, brought it up close to her face and, eye-to-eye, she "talked" to it in a cheeping babble while gently stroking its head with her forefinger. She punctuated her babble with question-and-exclamation nuances and soothing murmurs. It was a primitive lullaby with chirping lyrics.

After a moment or two of bonding, to teach it to eat and drink Mother first dipped the chick's beak in water, then in seed specially milled for newly hatched birds. Those with birth defects, or who appeared weaker than the rest, were separated from the flock and put in a protected corner to prevent the stronger ones from pecking them to death. Once the weather warmed up, those with birth defects were transferred to the smokehouse to be cared for by Joe and me. The producer bought these at a lesser price than the rest because only parts of the bird could be sold.

Mother worked in the turkey pens at least four hours a day. Her hands were chapped raw with huge knotted blood veins. And yet she refused to take off her wedding and engagement rings. But at some time during this second turkey season, her rings each broke in two or three places from the rough work. Her work-ravaged hands symbolized for me her devotion to her family and determination to work as hard as it took to care for us. Her fingernails bitten to the quick were an indication of the constant stress she felt.

Great-Granny Watts was in residence at her house and came to care for the feverish Joy during the day while Mother labored in the turkey pens. Great-Granny sat on the porch swing all day long with the fretful baby. Joy was no better the next day or the next. By the fourth day, Great-Granny admitted she dreamed all night long that she was swinging on the porch.

Great-Granny and Mother and Joy bonded during the week as the two women struggled to help Joy recover from her mysterious malady. "One day, Granny, when I have a nice house, you're going to live with me. You'll never have to pack your suitcase again," Mother swore to Great-Granny.

Before the fever developed, Joy had been in the initial stages of standing up and holding onto the bars of the crib. On the fourth evening after Great-Granny went home, Mother was sitting on the porch swing with Joy and stood her on her lap. The baby put her weight on both legs and then raised her left leg, screaming in agony.

Our father was pressed into turkey duty the next morning, while Granddaddy and Mother took Joy to our family doctor, Dr. Neighbors, who had no idea what was causing the problem and referred them to a specialist, the first of several. He X-rayed Joy's left leg from the knee down and diagnosed rickets. "You're supplementing breast milk with unpasteurized cow's milk and not giving the baby any orange juice," he declared. Mother tried explaining that orange juice gave Joy a rash, but the doctor refused to listen. He offered no explanation for the fever or severe pain. His diagnosis was obviously colored by his perception of our poverty.

Over the next week, Granddaddy chauffeured Mother and a feverish Joy to a number of doctors' offices, where they sat for hours waiting to see someone who might be able to help Joy. One or two doctors admitted they had no diagnosis, but offered pain medication for the present, and a wheelchair for when Joy outgrew her crib.

A drive to Austin was a special event in our family, and to make it several days in a row indicated the severity of Joy's illness and everyone's desperation to get her healthy again.

The trio finally wound up in Dr. Tisdale's office. He X-rayed Joy's entire left leg and discovered the hip socket was missing. "I'm not sure what we're going to do about this, but we have to do something," he declared. He took Joy's medical records with him to every medical convention he attended until she reached majority.

His theory was that Joy had had a sore throat early in September. Once the minor illness had run its course, the germs that should have been voided landed in her hip socket and ate away the bone. From the vantage point of the 21st century, I would guess it was a failure of her autoimmune system.

The Iron Lung Sorority

It took six adults in the hospital to hold Joy down while the needle from a large syringe was pushed through her left hip to withdraw pus from the space originally occupied by the hip socket. Mother and Joy were in the hospital for a week on the polio floor.

Back home in her crib, Joy spent the next six weeks in traction. She wasn't fully weaned, and Mother nursed her through the bars of the crib.

When Mother and Joy were in the hospital, I began to have foreboding dreams about my sister being threatened by an anonymous group of faceless people. I was always powerless to protect her from this dark, menacing force.

Joe was left to his own devices while Joy was ailing. He wandered happily over the secret recesses of the Holcomb Place, trailed by the pony-sized dogs our father used for herding cattle.

Mother tackled the laundry one Saturday shortly after Joy's release from the Austin hospital. I hung around to talk and lend a hand. In the course of the conversation, she reassured me that Joy would survive her illness. I was flooded with relief from a worry I hadn't acknowledged, and the nightmares stopped.

Agnes was a high-school friend of Mother's who lived not far from us. A devout Catholic, she gave birth to a baby a year. Mother fretted that her friend was ruining her health in service to a male-dominated faith. In retrospect, I'm sure Agnes also had her reservations regarding Mother's lifestyle. Although the two never got to visit in person, they sometimes offered each other moral support over the phone, despite the eavesdroppers on the party line.

I was privy to one of these sessions shortly after Mother and Joy returned from the hospital. Mother confided, "There's no sound like that of an iron lung being rolled down a hospital corridor. All the women with children on that floor shared a special bond. When we heard it coming, everyone walked to the door of their child's room to see where it was headed.

"There was one woman who only visited her child once or twice a day while the rest of us were there all the time. Her heels were just a little higher, her makeup a little heavier, and her hysteria a little greater every time she came. All the nurses and other mothers and even her own child were relieved when she left."

School Starts

While Mother and Granddaddy and Great-Granny Watts were struggling with Joy, I was running amock in the early weeks of first grade. The woman standing in front of the room started the first day of our formal educations with, "Good morning, boys and girls. I'm your teacher Mrs.

Turner. You're going to have to be especially good this year because I'm going through The Change." Most of the class was in shock from being away from home and our mothers for the first time and had no idea what she meant, but we didn't see much of her that year.

There was heavy dew on the ground that first day. The building was 1930s vintage. Huge metal slides were attached to various windows in lieu of fire escapes. Another very rusty slide on the playground was used as originally intended. Wearing my best dress for this most auspicious day, I broke ranks before school for just one slide. That evening, Mother spent hours with vinegar and lemon and salt and variations of the three ingredients in a struggle to remove the rust from the back of my dress. The lecture I received equaled the one she had delivered when I had left Joe wading in the clay.

A daily routine was established that first day and continued throughout the rest of our years on the Holcomb Place. I dressed and made my bed and choked down some hot cereal. Our father drove me to the general store in Cedar Creek, where I caught the school bus with others from the same general area.

There were two boys almost exactly my age in the community. One, born in February, was a rough-and-tumble regular little cowboy sort of boy while the other was an only child with a May birthday and artistic leanings. He could color neatly between the lines, draw beautiful pictures, and was considered a child prodigy when he competed in the local flower-arranging competition. The three of us were assigned the same teacher.

We had one substitute teacher after another during the year. Mrs. Turner was back for brief periods only now and again. She did phone Mother early in the year to compliment her on my vocabulary and to ask if I was an only child. Mother assumed I was acting like a spoiled brat. Looking back, I think the woman was considering retirement and wanted to know just how many more children like me were out there.

I was not an attractive child. Both knees and at least one elbow were always skinned. I chewed my fingernails past the quick. I found the boys to be much more fun than the girls and spent most every recess playing tag with them. At the end of the half-hour, my sash would be untied and my skirt pulled away from the waistband where someone had tried to tag me. My hair was always a mess as a result of Mother's home permanents. I attracted grass stains and dirt smudges as a magnet attracts metal filings. For one regrettable period, I had a boil on the end of my nose.

I had a habit of licking my lips, resulting in great chapped areas from my nose to my chin. Our father referred to me as "Liver Lips." His tone was not endearing.

The rough-and-tumble boy from Cedar Creek was one of my favorite tag companions. The artistic child usually met me at the door at the end of recess and tried to restore some semblance of order to my appearance as we returned to class.

Elementary Etiquette

Miss Arbuckle taught the other section of first grade and was regarded as an institution by many in the community. When our school year started, several parents with children assigned to Mrs. Turner's class protested. They had been students of Miss Arbuckle's and wanted their children to have her as well. Apparently, this was an annual diplomatic impasse that had to be negotiated by the Superintendent of Schools.

Mrs. Turner was replaced by substitutes more than half the school year. This left Miss Arbuckle with an unseasoned colleague to share playground duty. Most of the little boys and I were a rowdy lot.

During one momentous recess, Miss Arbuckle pulled me back from the entrance to the boys' restroom. I was on the verge of entering that sacrosanct sanctuary to continue the challenge an older boy had issued me on the playground. He had retreated there to save face when he realized he was about to be soundly beaten. I was determined to give him the thrashing he so richly deserved and was not to be deterred by decorum.

She took me aside to give me a lecture about being a lady. We both knew it was a waste of time and breath. I was not ready to be a lady. She probably knew the reputation of my McDaniel grandparents and didn't expect me to ever be one.

Floyd Martin drove the school bus and owned one of the three general stores in downtown Cedar Creek. He required the Mexican children to sit in the back of the bus and the white kids in the front. (The Black children attended a separate facility; I don't know if they had bus service or not.) My behavior on the bus was even less acceptable than during recess at school. I have always suffered from motion sickness and lost my hot cereal breakfast in the bus on the way to school on more than one occasion.

To help me learn the value of money, I was given a nickel each day to buy myself a treat during recess after lunch. It took me almost half the school year to learn how to keep track of the nickel until noon.

Jerry Mac Alexander was the favorite of everyone on the bus. Jerry was a polio victim. He was paralyzed from the waist down and "walked" by planting his crutches and swinging his braced legs forward. But Jerry had a sunny disposition and would frequently lead sing-alongs on the ride home.

He reported to his mother, my Granny Ellis's best friend, that I provided the daily comic relief with my inability to keep track of my nickel or my breakfast. The older children must have also noticed the scrapes and scratches I collected each day as well as my disheveled appearance at the end of the day. That's the way you earn a reputation in a small community.

I would never be a model student in terms of deportment, but once I was reassured that Joy was going to survive her illness, my overall grades greatly improved. I was always in the advanced reading group.

An Offer We Could Refuse

It was at least 9 p.m. I had been in bed over an hour and woke up when our father came home. The sound of Mother warming his supper probably woke me. The weather was cold, forcing the entire family to sleep in the main room for warmth.

Our father broke the usual silence, "Ginny, I ran into Uncle Lee in Cedar Creek this morning. He and Aunt Julia would like to take custody of Joy. They can't have a baby of their own and want one something terrible. They have more money than we do and can afford the finest care for her. He offered their house and some land in exchange. I told him the decision is up to you, but you need to realize this could be our opportunity to really get ahead."

There was a brief silence. I held my breath. Mother never answered. In a moment or two, our father made another remark on a different topic as though the first had never taken place. Mother must have given him a blistering look.

I went back to sleep weak with relief. Had Joy been "traded" to our relatives, regardless of their good intentions, it would have created an in irreparable division in our family. There would always have been a hole in our family where Joy belonged.

Teacher's Gift

Mrs. Gore was in our classroom in December. In the midst of caring for a seriously ill infant and thousands of delicate turkey chicks, Mother managed to find the time to bake a date loaf cake as a gift for my teacher. She wrapped it in tin foil and tied it with a thin red ribbon.

Date Loaf Cake

Chop 1 (8-ounce) package of dates and 1 cup pecans. Add 2 teaspoons soda and 2 cups boiling water. Stir and set aside to cool.

In the meantime, cream 2 cups sugar with 2/3 cup shortening. Add 2 eggs, one at a time, and then the cooled pecan/date mixture. Blend in 3 cups all-purpose flour and bake in a greased and floured tube pan in a preheated 325° oven for one hour. Cool completely.

Icing

1 cup brown sugar
4 tablespoons cream
1 piece of butter about the size of a walnut

Mix these ingredients together and then spread over cake. It will be thin.

SCHOOL DAYS 1952 - '53
Bastrop

This is my first-grade school picture. This is the same dress I was wearing when I slid down the wet, rusty slide on the first day of school, so Mother must have been able to remove all the rust. Note the sharp creases ironed in the sleeves.

If Joy had been just a bit older when she got sick, Great-Granny Watts would probably have made her an egg custard. She thought it was good for anything from a cold to cancer.

Egg Custard

2 cups whole milk
2 tablespoons all-purpose flour
1 teaspoon vanilla

3 beaten eggs
1 tablespoon butter
1 cup sugar

Heat the milk until it's just about to boil before adding the other ingredients. Pour custard ingredients in a buttered ovenproof dish. Set dish in a larger pan. Add water to the pan. The custard should bake about approximately 30 minutes while standing in about 1 ½" of water. It's done when a tester is inserted in the center and comes out clean.

—CHAPTER SEVEN—

The A & A General Store

Cedar Creek was the closest settlement to the Holcomb Place. It had originally been a center for lumbering as well as farming and ranching, but the timber trade was no longer part of the local economy by the early 1950s.

The most imposing residence was Mrs. Sophie Smith's two-storied clapboard house, which had supposedly served as an inn for the stagecoach line in a much earlier time. Next to it were two or three asbestos-shingled houses with chain-link fences surrounding front yards of smooth bare dirt interspersed with an occasional patch of St. Augustine grass.

There were three general stores with gas pumps outside. Although the resident children were bussed to Bastrop for school, the old one-room schoolhouse still stood across the Farm-to-Market Road from the stores and was used for community gatherings. The small white-steeple church was located a block or so down the road from the commercial center of the community.

The majority of the Caucasians living in and around Cedar Creek were of Scotch- Irish descent. They had known each other for generations. Most families were inter-related, or had known each other so long they were treated like family.

We were a fair-skinned people. The men wore Stetson

hats constantly but still had dark red, almost purple necks from continuous exposure to the sun. We were Rednecks before it became a recognized social status. On the rare occasion when a man removed his hat, a permanent indentation in his hair could be seen where his Stetson rested.

Pickups and other larger trucks were the most popular means of transportation. Sedans were impractical. Guns were considered a dangerous tool. Most trucks had a gun rack hanging across the back window for safe transportation of a rifle or two. A coil of rope might also hang from an empty hook behind the seat.

We were hugely proud of being independent and being Texan and of having worked hard to earn what little we had. No one ever talked much about the Civil War. I'm not sure they were aware that most of our poverty was a direct result of Reconstruction, which had pretty effectively stolen our fair share of the American dream. The code and lifestyle of the old West was the major influence on our community. We were proud of living in the largest state in the nation and far from despairing of our isolation, we savored it.

J.A. Martin's General Store was the center of the community. J. A. and his father before him served the general public and extended limited credit. The Cedar Creek post office was located in his store, making its front porch a natural gathering spot for the men of the community.

Floyd Martin's General Store faced the Farm-to-Market Road that cut through Cedar Creek and was almost exactly back–to–back with J.A.'s. The building had originally been Floyd's father's blacksmith shop. As previously mentioned, Floyd also drove the school bus to supplement his income.

Across the road from J.A. Martin's store was the A & A General Store that had been established by some of our Wamel and Alexander relatives a couple of generations back to serve their hired hands. The workers were paid partly in cash and partly in credit at the store. Some would also be provided housing in shacks located on their employers' land.

Our father bought this store the fall I started school and Joy got sick. Granny moved her treadle Singer sewing machine to the A & A and assumed management. Until I married, she made every stitch of clothing our family wore, with the exception of blue jeans. There's no doubt it was a huge undertaking, but she made the most out of it by posing as a semi-martyr. Whenever I would appear in a new garment, someone would remark on how lucky I was to have such a talented and generous grandmother. It wasn't really that great. She was reimbursed for the materials she used, and we rarely had any input in the selection of either the fabric or the pattern. The rare dress she made for Mother would always have been better suited to an elderly woman.

Our father and I would drive into Cedar Creek and open the A & A before I caught the school bus into Bastrop. Granddaddy would bring Granny to relieve him in an hour or so for him to feed his animals, check fences and tend to the countless other farming and ranching chores. At the end of the day, the bus would drop me off at the store, where I would stay with Granny until our father returned at five to close the store and take us home.

The two hours from the time the bus dropped me off at the store until closing time often felt like a month. Granny thought little girls should be able to just sit and do nothing.

The Outcasts

There were a number of local families bearing the Martin surname who didn't seem to be related. Floyd Martin turned the management of his store over to another man named Martin who took up residence in the back of the store. He brought along a woman who wasn't his wife and her six children. Granny's position was clear. "I know there are children playing across the road, but you will not associate with those trashy people. That man over there drinks and beats them. Mrs. Bob Turner heard them talking on the party line last week. The baby fell against the heater and burned himself pretty bad. The other children were up all night trying to keep him from crying and waking the man. He would have beaten the burned child for disturbing his sleep. Just come out on the porch and sit with me."

I dragged myself out through the double-screen doors of the store and, deeply bored, sat beside Granny on the narrow bench next to the building's front wall. The store had been built on a slight rise, with the front of the building higher off the ground than the back. Three or four steps were required to reach the front porch from the road. The view from the bench was partially blocked by two gasoline pumps between the porch and the gravel road.

My gaze first rested on the far distance. It was only after my bottom began to get sore from sitting that I happened to look down at the road and at the weed-choked empty lot directly across the road. Two or three of the children Granny had forbidden me to associate with were mutely seated cross-legged among the weeds staring at Granny and me. I made an excuse about homework and went inside the store.

The differences between those children and my siblings and me were a matter of public perception. They were newcomers. Our father's ancestors had lived in the area for at least three generations. Great-Granddaddy Watts's younger brother, Otto Wamel, helped build the church. The Ellis and Watts families had earned respectable reputations. Our father often announced, "I'm an honest and good person." We had no reason not to believe him.

The Martins who managed Floyd's general store were regarded as undesirable for three reasons: their mother wasn't married to the man they were living with; he drank; and he abused the children. The Martins lived in the back of the general store in the middle of the community and talked freely about their personal life on the party line.

In sharp contrast, we lived miles away on a remote piece of property where Mother rarely used the phone for fear of offending her mother-in-law. We were always closely supervised by our parents and other family members on the rare occasions we were out in public. Our beatings always took place in the privacy of our home, with only Mother and our pets as witnesses. We lived in constant fear of our father's next explosion. There was never any warning. It made social misfits of us. Nervous anticipation made us socially clumsy. We made jokes that weren't funny and tried too hard to be accommodating to everyone.

James was one of the eldest Martin children and a classmate of mine. He was in the lowest reading circle, and the substitute teacher displayed a disdainful attitude towards him, but James was always kind to me. When he chased me in tag, he played fair and didn't try to grab at my sash or skirt to tag me. His clothes were shabby and his hair too long and sometimes greasy. James never had a nickel for a lunch treat or a quarter to buy the hot lunch. His limp lunch sack usually held a few crackers and some sad-looking rat cheese. James and I had much more in common than outward appearances would indicate.

Public Relations Miscalculation

The first spring our family owned the A & A our father came across a nest of rattlesnakes on the Holcomb Place and killed five or six really large ones. He was so impressed with their size that he strung the bodies on wire and hung the wire across the iron bars of one of the front windows of the store for everyone in the community to see.

That fall when he needed help working his cattle, branding and de-horning and castrating the calves, he couldn't get any of the usual Colored men he hired to help. They had all seen the snakes hanging from the window. Having decided the Holcomb Place was snake-infested, people were afraid to work there.

The A & A was a long, narrow building of weathered boards. The parking-lot side was covered with metal signs that would be weathered enough by the '70s to decorate a fern bar. A set of double doors graced the exact center of both the front and parking-lot sides of the building. A supply of bagged cattle feed was kept in the back of the store. Pickup trucks were backed to the side door for easier loading of bagged feed and other bulky purchases.

I only remember our father sitting shop one weekday afternoon. It was cold enough that day for me to wear my dress wool coat outside to play. Someone earlier in the day had backed their truck into the well at the far end of the parking lot. Big concrete fragments were scattered among the weeds. I was unaware of the recent accident and ran through the weeded area for the love of running.

I tripped over one piece of concrete and hit my nose on another. The pain was the worst I'd ever known. Blood gushed from my nose. Our father came running when he heard my screams, picked me up, carried me inside, and ministered to my wound by sticking cotton up my nose. It was the only one-on-one interaction I ever had with the man that did not end in either physical or verbal abuse. It was almost worth the blood stains on my red wool coat.

Ornery Visitors

There was a potbellied stove in the dead center of the store set in a metal box to keep it from burning the floor. We were in the middle of a severe cold snap. The weather was too bad to spend any time outside unless it was absolutely necessary. Our Great-Granddaddy Watts's baby brother, Otto Wamel, wandered in to while away some time. (I'm not sure how many "greats" I'd have to put in front of his name to correctly indicate our relationship.) He enjoyed a reputation for being perhaps just a little more than a social drinker. Granny pursed her lips when he walked in the door.

Her lips got even tighter and her back straighter and more rigid when Si Simmons entered the store exclaiming, "I found a dollar bill in my jeans pocket this morning that I didn't know I had." Granny had told me Mr. Simmons was "born tired," a euphemism for being lazy. He was a frequent occupant of J. A. Martin's front porch.

He had come to visit with Uncle Otto, who was his brother-in-law. Uncle Otto replied, "I knew it had to be something special. I haven't seen you look so pleased with yourself since my wedding night when I crawled into bed expecting to cuddle up with Laura and found you there instead. By the way, you have the boniest butt in the county."

"You've been saying that for almost fifty years," answered Mr. Simmons. "It couldn't have happened to a more deserving scoundrel. I believe that was the best shiveree I ever attended."

"Attended? You know you planned the whole thing!" said Uncle Otto accusingly. At about that moment, Granny dropped her scissors. We all turned at the clatter to be hit with an icy stare. The two men laughed and clapped each other on the back. They were bored on this cold day and had come to the store to enjoy each other's company and give Granny a hard time.

I had already eaten my afternoon snack. It was too cold to send me outside to play. My homework was done. Granny was stuck. There was nothing she could use to distract me from these two, who were plainly there to be a naughty influence.

Simon Simmons is my favorite name. I've always wondered what possessed his parents to hang that combination on a newborn. I also wonder if they were aware of the semi-play on words in the combination. Imagine a little boy, tongue lolling as he concentrates on learning to write his name and put all those "M's" in the proper order.

Family Gossip

"You know, Jackie Lee," said Uncle Otto. "My mother was married to a man in Kentucky before she came to Texas. His name was William Warfield Watts. I think it's fair to say Momma had a weakness for the letter W. Anyway, they had been married several years and your great-grandpa was a little boy when all of a sudden her husband just disappeared. In a week or two, her sister ran away from home. Momma was an unwilling participant in a frontier divorce. They didn't have lawyers back then or judges anywhere handy. If you weren't happy in your marriage, the only way out was to disappear.

"It was hard back then for a woman to support herself, especially with a child. So Momma decided to move to Texas for a fresh start. They took the train to Texas and somewhere along the way at a rest stop, your great-grandpa managed to get kicked in the face by a mule. He had to stay for over a year with the doctor in that little whistle-stop to try and get his jaw healed. It never would, and they wound up removing it, along with his bottom teeth.

"He had joined Momma in Texas by the time he was eleven and working with a teamster moving cattle to market when Momma met my daddy, and they married. A few years later, when I was toddling around another family named Watts moved to Bastrop County. Sure enough, it was Momma's first husband and her sister and two or three little kids.

"Momma had a choice: she could shoot him like he deserved, or she could just ignore him. She decided to ignore him and leave him to the mercy of his own conscience. Besides, she knew the two of them and figured they deserved each other.

"You know, your great grandpa had the most colorful vocabulary of anyone around. With his jaw messed up, he had a speech impediment, but working with the teamsters, he learned a few of the more colorful phrases."

"Yes," added Mr. Simmons. "He was the only man who could get away with cussin' around women. Even they thought he was funny."

Granny was saved from further aggravation by the arrival of our father. He was warmly greeted by the two elderly men who happily made room for him in the circle around the stove.

"Gordon, we were just telling Jackie Lee about her Great-Granddaddy Watts," said Uncle Otto.

Our father smiled, "My favorite story about him is the time he heard something out in the chicken house in the middle of the night and went running out to check on the hens carrying his shotgun and wearing a long nightshirt and his hat and his boots, his handlebar mustache flying behind him."

"Did he really teach you to swim by tying a rope around your waist and throwing you in the stock tank?" asked Mr. Simmons.

"Oh, yes." Our father nodded and ruefully laughed.

Wrapped in Butcher Paper and Tied in String

Later that spring, when the weather warmed up, I returned to the store after school one day to find Granny deeply engrossed in a project. In front of her, she had a case of boxes labeled "Kotex." She took each individual box, wrapped it in butcher paper and tied it with string. It took her all afternoon. She then stacked them beneath the old wind-up cash register under the counter rather than on a shelf. I didn't dare ask about this for fear of getting my ears boxed again.

However, shortly thereafter, it came to my attention that the young women in the community who did not ordinarily patronize our store were coming to purchase these boxes from Granny. Since she was the only female clerk in any of the stores, I decided this had to be a "girl thing." But why couldn't she stack the bare boxes on a back shelf and when one was purchased, place it in a paper bag? The butcher paper and string seemed almost as obvious as the naked box. Adults, go figure!

A Pox on Coon Hunting

I felt really sick at school in the middle of the day. The diagnosis was chicken pox. Duval, the hired man, had to come get me. Joe and Joy also succumbed to the malady within the next few days. All three of us were in the worst stage of the illness together. On one evening in particular, Mother had a terrible time getting three feverish, itchy children to sleep.

Just after we had drifted off and she was about to crawl into bed, a terrible racket broke out in our back yard. Something started thumping and bumping under the house. All three of us were awakened by the chaos. Our father hurriedly slipped on his clothes to go outside. Several "coon hunters" and their dogs had cornered some wild critter under our house. He didn't go out to reprimand them for disturbing his sick children. He had several relatives and even more friends who were coon hunters. He was curious to see if he knew any of these men and to see what they had been chasing.

I have as little understanding of coon hunting as of NASCAR and even less appreciation. From what little I've been able to gather on the subject, the object is for a number of men to meet out in the middle of nowhere, build a camp fire, and turn their dogs loose to see what they can find to chase. The time spent waiting is usually occupied with passing libations around the fire and generally communing with nature. I'm not really clear on how they catch up with the dogs once something is treed.

Mother's major shortcoming was that she was entirely too nice and polite to everyone. She should have gone out and "treed" every man for waking her babies.

Joe and Joy

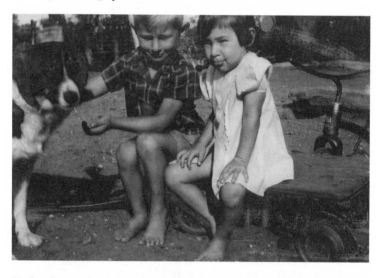

My brother and sister were consulted in the composition of this memoir, and this is the only point upon which we cannot agree. According to Joe, our Aunt Mac took this candid snapshot the summer before he started school. Joy swears the little girl is me. I'm equally sure it's Joy. It doesn't really matter. We have always closely resembled each other. The little girl's facial expression is a prime example of the family lip. The lower lip is fully extended and quivers slightly any time we feel we're the target of injustice. One of my daughters and a grandson have inherited "The Lip."

The children are sitting on the wagon that our father ran over and Granddaddy repaired by replacing the bent bed with a sturdy board. It turned out to be a happy accident, because it made it easier for Joy to get on and off the wagon when she had to wear the rocker-shaped brace.

The subjects of this photograph are obviously not happy. This was apparently one of those unfortunate photo opportunities where the children are caught misbehaving and then required to smile for the camera. It must have been a minor misdemeanor since none of us can recall exactly what happened. Also, notice how well-fed and happy the dog looks.

During those three years when I was the only child in the family in school, Joe and Joy forged a special bond. My brother inherited a strong nurturing instinct from both his grandfathers and always took a special interest in Joy. Once they were both in school, the bus driver told Mother that Joe always got off the bus first and stood waiting for Joy to disembark before turning away to start walking home with his little sister beside him.

Mother made a point each evening over dinner to ask what I had learned at school that day. One night in third grade, I regaled her with the chapter about farming families in the Midwest we'd covered in social studies that day. According to the description of an average family day, the mother *in her spare time* would spend an occasional afternoon plowing on the tractor. That really irritated Mother on two different counts. In the first place, she had no spare time and in the second, in Texas, only the most desperately poverty-stricken families had their womenfolk out working in the fields.

—CHAPTER EIGHT—

Christmas, 1952

It was early December 1952. Mother and our father had taken Joy to see Dr. Tisdale. All the adults in our family were tremendously anxious about this checkup. The doctors hadn't been sure how to treat her condition. Enough time had now passed to determine if they were on the right track.

It was a school day, and the bus dropped me off as usual at the A & A to join Granny. Granddaddy had kept Joe with him while our parents went for this appointment. The two of them were also at the store when I arrived. This is the only time I remember Granddaddy being in the A & A.

He behaved out of character the entire afternoon. When our parents pulled up in the parking lot, our usually reserved grandfather ran out to the truck, grabbed open the passenger's door, snatched Joy from Mother's lap and held her tightly to his chest for a long hug. Granddaddy was not usually this demonstrative. None of us knew how to react to this outburst.

His behavior makes perfect sense in retrospect. J. C. Ellis lost his first son to a sudden, inexplicable illness. He had probably been afraid since the onset of Joy's illness that we were going to lose her too. We were lucky this time. The doctor gave Joy a good report. We could look forward to a carefree Christmas.

A Mournful Holiday

My last day of school before the Christmas holiday was a half-day. There was a gift swap and a school-wide assembly of Christmas carols. I was awash in the Christmas spirit. A neighbor gave me a ride from Cedar Creek to my gate, and I walked to the house. I was looking forward to the community Christmas party planned at the Old School House that evening.

Everyone was bringing food. Mother had been baking for days. Canned tuna had recently been introduced at the general store. Mother made tuna-salad sandwiches and added pecans. She was excited about the new product. "The sandwiches taste just like chicken salad," she gushed.

The day was overcast. Joe and I were playing on the uneven floor in front of the fireplace that provided most of the light for the room and heat for the room, and Joy was bouncing up and down in her crib. The phone on the kitchen wall rang. Mother answered. She spoke in a low voice for quite a while.

I know that she then told us that Granddaddy was dead, but I don't recall the words she used. We had been completely sheltered from death. When Minnie Pearl died, Mother had put off telling me for weeks until I'd grown accustomed to the cat's absence. But this time she had no choice; we would shortly be forced to face the realities of our grieving father and the funeral.

That morning, Granny's brother, T. C. Watts, had needed help with a sick cow and had gone to get Granddaddy. At first he didn't notice that Dusty wasn't saddled and tethered to the tree beside the dining room window as usual. He found Granddaddy seated in a rocking chair in the back bedroom with his two dogs resting on either side.

It was a small room. The double bed with its painted metal frame and feather bed-mattress filled one corner next to a window. There was a floor-model radio at the end of the bed. A rocking chair was angled between the foot of the bed and the fireplace.

Granddaddy was seated in the rocker. His dogs, Butchie and Fido, were resting on either side of the chair. He had shot himself behind the right ear. The bullet had gone through his head at an upward angle and ricocheted off the ceiling and one wall before landing between his feet. There was no note.

An Open Casket

They took us to the funeral home the next night. It was an open casket. The men, dressed in suits with clumsily tied ties and without their Stetsons, looked completely vulnerable. This heightened the severity of the occasion. I was frightened by the sight of their faces swollen and red from weeping or the effort not to.

It is one thing to be told someone has died and another entirely to see it for the first time. Reality set in when I saw the body. "Granddaddy, you can't leave us!" I howled.

One of our father's aunts carried me to the back of the room to sit on a sofa. There was another copy of that Jim Crow image of Christ hanging over the coffin. She explained that Granddaddy had gone to be with Christ. That was all well and good for Christ, but we needed Granddaddy at home. Christ had lots of people. We only had one Granddaddy.

A cousin-in-law of one of Granny's sisters stayed with us at the sister's house on Burnet Road in Austin the next day while the adults attended the funeral and burial. Fearful that funeral expenses would preclude purchases for Santa, Granddaddy's brother Elmo bought us especially nice toys to entertain us. The xylophone pull toy he gave Joy was a huge hit with her and Joe. Our sitter, a maiden-lady schoolteacher, had a major stress headache, but never mentioned it the entire time Joe and Joy chased each other and pulled that clanging toy around and around the interior of the house from the living room to the dining room to the kitchen and from there to the master bedroom, over the floor furnace and down the hall to the living room again.

The family gathered back at Great-Granny Watts's house after the services. There was one awful moment when someone noticed the holster for the gun Granddaddy used was still hanging in its usual place on the back porch. The men caring for the body and cleaning the room had thrown the antique pistol in the Colorado but had overlooked the holster.

"Just So" Comfort

For the rest of December, we lived at Great-Granny's, where we spent the holidays entertaining a steady stream of condolence callers. Blue-haired ladies with sparse, bristly black mustaches would hurriedly ask for lurid details any time Granny left the room. There was an unmistakable gleam of excitement in their eyes. Some almost drooled.

Granny never decorated for Christmas. It was too much trouble. Mother made a point to order our Christmas toys when the Sears catalog was first distributed in September. This holiday our toys were left for us at the foot of our bed on a chair.

I woke well before dawn on Christmas morning. It was bitterly cold. I had to wait for the others to wake before investigating what Santa had brought. I sleepily watched the toys on the chair taking shape in the growing light of the dawn. My favorite gift was a copy of Rudyard Kipling's *Just So Stories*. I love his alliteration. His reference to the "great, gray-green, greasy Limpopo River all hung about with fever trees" is my favorite example. In retrospect, I should have paid closer attention to the example set by the independent Elephant's Child, who marches to his own beat despite family disapproval.

Major holidays were always celebrated with a huge dinner for the extended family. It usually took three seatings to serve everyone. The men and children were fed first, and then the women took turns eating and doing the dishes.

Granny's Grief

We moved back to the Holcomb Place when school started. Granny began a frenzy of cleaning and rearranging.

She burned all Granddaddy's belongings, including his complete collection of several Western romances.

Then she put out poison without giving any reason. Fido, Granddaddy's big yellow hound, just disappeared. The little bulldog, Butchie, showed up at our house frothing at the mouth. Mother was able to force enough bacon grease down his throat to save him. I can't imagine why, but our father took him back to Granny. He showed up a few days later in the same condition. This time he was too weak for Mother to save. She spent a half hour in weeping hysteria on the phone with the party-line operator. They tried calling everyone they could think of for help, but to no avail.

Mother said Butchie came to us because he knew we loved Granddaddy as much as he did and would help him. In my childish mind, I understood he didn't realize his master was dead and thought if Granddaddy would come back, it would be to see us.

Fido and Butchie had been faithful companions and deserved more respect than they received. It gave me some small comfort to think of the three together in the afterlife. I will never understand why Granny didn't have T. C. shoot the dogs or give them away.

This was the pivotal experience of my life. Not a day has passed since that I've not thought of this man and mourned his loss. Now that Joe and Joy and I are all older than Granddaddy was when he chose to end his life, we have a better perspective on why he did it.

Shortly after it happened, I decided he shot the wrong person. I used to think that if he had shot Granny instead, not a jury in the county would have convicted him. They would probably have given him a medal and declared his birthday a special holiday.

Of course, that's not true. Granddaddy loved his wife. When they were courting, he accidentally drowned his horse in a swollen stream in his rush to visit her. He was devoted to Granny. He shaved her legs for her and helped her pull on her Longline girdle for dressy occasions. There was tangible proof of this: in the struggle to yank it up, he poked his finger through the garment in a rather indelicate place. (There can be no secrets when an extended family lives under the same roof and shares a communal clothesline.)

I realize, as an adult, that Granny and Granddaddy both suffered from depression. He expressed his illness with one final desperate act, while she made us all miserable for years with her mean and angry behavior.

Sleeping in a Feather Bed

Great-Granny Watts's bedroom was the first door on the right just inside the front door in the center of the house. It was one of the few rooms in the house in which the splintery wood floor was covered in a dark nondescript linoleum. I remember it as a small square room with a fireplace directly opposite the door. The smallest closet I've ever seen was set into the wall to the right of the fireplace.

A tall golden oak chest with deep drawers faced the back of the door as it swung open. Its drawers were the deepest of my experience and impossible for a child to open. They always stuck at odd angles. A square table stood beside the chest and in front of the window facing the front porch. This window and the matching one in my grandparents' bedroom were tall and low to the floor, making it possible to easily step from the bedroom to the porch, but the screen prevented any imaginative exits.

A lamp stood in the center of the table, providing light for Great-Granny's continuous handwork. Her delicate stitches surrounded every buttonhole in all our clothing until age diminished her skill.

Her bed took up most of the room to the left of the door. The head and footboards were metal and painted a dull brown. A once-brightly colored floral arrangement was painted in the wide section of the middle of the headboard.

A smaller window was cut into the wall at the foot of the bed. Unscreened, it opened onto the back screened-in porch. The rest of the wall space beyond the short window was filled by a marble-topped washstand that matched the chest of drawers.

A white enamel washbasin was kept on top of the washstand with a matching chamber pot on the floor at the foot of the bed.

A small pendulum clock in the center of the mantle with Great-Granny's sewing basket beside it and a small radio on the table by the lamp were the only other accessories in the room.

From a child's viewpoint, Great-Granny's bed was merely spectacular. It had a feather mattress. Sturdy boards were used as slats to support the springs and mattress. The side pieces of the bedframe had a shelf on the inner side approximately 1½ in. to 2 in. wide, where the slats fitted. The springs resting between the slats and mattress were bare and required occasional dusting.

The mattress was covered in the traditional mattress-ticking canvas and stuffed with feathers. My memory fails me. I have no idea what was used to protect the mattress from the bare springs.

The least pressure applied to the mattress left an indentation. You didn't lie down on a feather mattress; it enveloped you. In winter, we slept with our heads up by the headboard, but switched ends in warm weather to catch any possible breeze from the windows. The feathers were a warm blessing in winter but smothering the rest of the year.

The mattress had to be picked up along one side and fluffed up with vigorous shaking before the sheets and quilts and chenille spread could be smoothed over and tucked around it. There was a real art to making a feather bed.

Sweet Memories

Mother made these cookies every Christmas.

Gumdrop Cookies

Beat the following together until fluffy:
1 cup shortening
1 cup brown sugar

1 cup granulated sugar
Add three eggs and beat thoroughly.
In a separate bowl, combine 2 cups all-purpose flour,
1 teaspoon soda, ¼ teaspoon salt. Combine with
sugar mixture and add the following:
2 cups oatmeal
1 cup coconut
1 cup chopped gumdrop candy
1 teaspoon vanilla

Drop walnut sizes of the dough on a cookie sheet and
bake at 350° for about eight minutes.

Makes about six dozen.

This is the way I like to think of Granddaddy Ellis. He's in his element
here with his horse and dog. The horse is as big a pet as the dog and
came willingly. There's another horse in the background headed toward
the group in the foreground to be petted.

The horse on the left has its mane cut short. I suspect this was done to keep the hairs out of the way while roping cows or calves from horseback. It would also make it easier to keep it free from stickers and burrs. The animals are obviously well fed, while the man is thin almost to the point of emaciation.

—CHAPTER NINE—

Desperate Times

Texas received 30 to 50 percent less rain than normal in the years from 1949 to 1957. The temperatures were also higher than average. Many of our teachers were married to farmers or ranchers, so the drought was a frequent topic of conversation at school, where the atmosphere was subdued. Requests for extra workbooks or other school supplies were kept to a minimum. There were no field trips.

School was dismissed for the summer at the end of May. The Cedar Creek Cemetery Association held its annual Homecoming at the old one-room schoolhouse on the last Sunday of that month. The atmosphere might have been somewhat more subdued that year and the contributions down a bit, but everyone came for a potluck luncheon after church.

Two or three waist-high tables, each about ten or fifteen yards long, were set parallel to each other with plenty of room between them for people to pass back and forth. A tin roof supported by raw cedar posts sheltered the tables. Each extended family would place their food in their own section of a table, but there was plenty of table hopping to get at least a bit of all the best offered.

The purpose of Homecoming was to raise money for the maintenance of the local cemeteries. There are two in

Cedar Creek: the Upper and the Lower. The Lower predated the 1836 Texas rebellion against Mexico. The caretakers declared it "full." They grew weary of digging graves there, only to find space already occupied. Disturbing an antique burial spot smacked of disrespect.

Granny was secretary-treasurer of the organization. The teacher's desk was brought out from the school and set up at one side. Granny sat behind it and accepted contributions. Contributors wore short lengths of ribbon pinned to their collars with straight pins indicating their participation in the fund drive. The money collected was spent on maintaining the cemeteries or was invested in a certificate of deposit for future maintenance.

Folding chairs were set up at one end of the tables for the elderly. Many of them were using cardboard fans with wooden handles and a picture of the square white school building on the cardboard stapled to the handle, with the slogan "I'm a fan of Cedar Creek." The others milling about all made a point of stopping to pay their respects to those pillars of the community who no longer had the strength to help in the production of the event.

In election years, all the candidates made a special point of attending Homecoming to solicit votes. The bankers from Bastrop always attended, as did some of the more prominent citizens, like Dr. Gordon Bryson, who delivered most of the Caucasian babies in the county.

Mother found a special spot for us close to Granny's desk. We sat on the crossbeams underneath the nearest table. Mother turned a cardboard box upside down for us to use as a table. We were tucked away in a safe spot where we could eat in peace and see everything and everyone and not get trampled by the adults. This was the last time we would leave the Holcomb Place until August.

Drought

The lack of rain was as hard on the morale of the farmers and ranchers as it was on their wallets. Our father was increasingly surly and short-tempered. I began to listen in the late afternoons for the rattle of the bridge that he would have to cross if he was going to be home in time for supper. If I heard it, I would find something to read and go get on my bed on the front porch.

He would drive past our front gate and on another couple of miles to visit with his mother before coming home for the evening. Granny had a dramatic personality and was always in the middle of her crisis *du jour*. Many of these were generated by perceived misconduct attributed to Mother or one of us. Our father invariably arrived home in a foul humor or a total rage.

It was diplomatic to be out of reach on my bed when he parked his truck by the back steps at the end of the day. All too often the child playing in the general vicinity of the back had his or her quiet play interrupted by heavy-handed swats and/or angry, sarcastic scolding. Since our parents had agreed that Joy's illness made spanking her out of the question, Joe was the one who usually bore the brunt of our father's wrath.

It was a challenge to amuse ourselves in that remote location. Santa had brought us a wagon with a wooden body over a metal frame. When our father accidentally backed over it, Granddaddy replaced the broken body with a flat piece of wood, which made it much easier for Joe to get Joy in the wagon and pull her. There were few places on our property they didn't explore.

Joy had spent most of the previous winter in a series of casts, and in the summer graduated to a special brace shaped like a rocker, fashioned from a rocking chair, with a shoe built on a swivel at each end. She quickly learned to walk by balancing on the middle of the rocker and could outrun Mother both up and down hill between the house and the turkey pen.

Joe and I learned to "walk the barrels." We took two old barrels from the barn, turned them on their side and learned to walk along the drive and around the yard, balancing on the rounded side of the barrel. You had to walk backwards to propel the barrel forward and vice versa.

The turkey roosts were slender cedar posts arranged like stadium seats. We swung from the higher posts and practiced "walking the tightrope" along the lower ones. An antique horse-drawn harvester had been turned on its side and abandoned in a small grove of scrub trees in back of the big turkey house. We climbed on the top wheel and enjoyed a brief partial spin.

One day I reclined in the fork of a short tree to read my favorite book, *Girl of the Limberlost*, and got so engrossed in the story that I fell out of the tree, tearing the last two pages out on the way down.

Fowl Bedlam

Two disreputable barrels cluttered the bare beaten earth of our backyard, along with our wagon and the bits and pieces from Joe's latest mechanical experiment, but they were the least offensive factor.

By spring, the turkeys had outgrown their pens and totally taken over the homestead. The first night they spent out on their own, a number of them wandered across our property and the Farm-to-Market Road to spend the night roosting on Andy Alexander's freshly painted white picket fence. Andy was Great-Granny Watts' first cousin. He was most understanding, but when the turkeys went to market, several wound up in the Alexanders' freezer in payment for the damages.

We were living in fowl bedlam. The hired hand, Duval, had built a six-foot-tall wire fence around the house in a futile attempt to give us some space away from the turkeys. Some of the birds habitually roosted in the scrub trees near the house. Before dawn they would fly over the fence and make their way from the ground to the back porch or the pickup and then to the roof. We would be awakened by the screech of claws sliding down the tin roof.

A turkey defecates approximately a tablespoon or so at a time of feces shaped like dollops of frosting piped out of a pastry bag. Mother raised three crops of turkeys. The first year there were 1,500; 3,000 the next and 5,000 the last year. It was impossible to avoid the turkey poop.

I heard a segment on National Public Radio some time ago on human longevity. The theory was that those people who are exposed to animals and babies live the longest. If there is any validity to this theory, Joe and Joy and I should set some sort of record.

As the summer progressed, the toms would become territorial and attacked us by flying down on us from the trees. They clawed us and beat us with their wings.

We also learned that turkeys are not the brightest of God's beasts. Early one summer morning, Mother had occasion to walk down to the smaller turkey house at the entrance to the homestead by the barn. The turkeys were all asleep on their roost in the house. A young bobcat was under the roost. He was having the time of his life grabbing sleeping turkeys from the perch one at a time to kill them and play with the carcass for a moment before grabbing another. Mother tiptoed away to return shortly with the .22 and put an end to the bobcat and its game.

Mother learned to shoot as a child when she went hunting with her father. Grandpa McDaniel had a motorcycle with a sidecar and would pack her in the sidecar along with his rifle and his big hairy dog with oversized ears and paws to match.

The dog had never seen the motorcycle without the sidecar and was accustomed to ride along on all occasions. He had no idea the sidecar could be unhooked, until one day when Grandpa needed to ride the motorcycle without his canine companion. The dog followed Grandpa from the house to the motorcycle, prancing all the way with "Hot Damn, we're goin' huntin'" body language, jumped in the sidecar, and assumed his favorite position, chin resting on the edge to catch the maximum breeze; then Grandpa revved up the motorcycle and pulled away, leaving dog and sidecar behind. The poor dog's demeanor instantly changed from excitement to dismay.

Animals (with the exception of turkeys) do talk. Most humans just don't listen.

The Cistern

Our father had started coming home for the noon meal in the heat of the day to hear the stock-market report over the radio and to nap for a while before going back out to work.

Lunch was always strained on the days he was home. He listened to the livestock market report over WOAI out of San Antonio as we ate, and he demanded total silence from us all. If you had anything to share with him, it was vital to do so before the report began.

This prompted Mother to share her concern with him the moment he walked in the back door. This was urgent. "Baby, the cistern water has tasted 'off' for several days, and now there are feathers floating in it. I think a turkey must have managed to wedge in the small opening at the top of the cistern and drowned in there."

He looked really peeved and said, "I'll call the County Ag Agent to see what he recommends." We were all appalled to hear that the expert suggested a large bottle of bleach be added to the tainted water. Our father complied, with revolting results. We were stuck drinking this until the following Sunday, when our father was home all day. After having nothing else available to drink for an entire day, he opened the spigot on the cistern to drain out the tainted water, and then ordered a fresh supply.

Cattle Feed

To stay solvent during the drought, our father had reduced his herd and settled on two unique solutions for supplementing bagged feed and hay for those remaining.

The Holcomb Place was covered with cacti as well as mesquite. Our father used a gadget called a "pear burner" to burn the thorns off the cacti. I cannot explain the mechanics of the gizmo. All I remember is that the operator wore a small butane tank on his back. There was a hose running from the tank to a narrow pipe about three feet long. The pipe ended in a nozzle. When it was turned on, a flame came out of the nozzle and was directed at the cacti leaves. It must have been a brutal chore in the summer's heat, but it provided a great source of food and moisture for the cattle.

Our father also bought cotton-seed hulls and served them in the cattle trough covered with molasses. The molasses softened the hulls enough for the cattle to chew them and made the cows' coats glisten.

Desolation

I came away from this period in my life with a unique definition of "bleak." My version of a bleak scene is rolling hills of parched earth with gray-green gnarled mesquite trees bent under a blazing sun. All the buildings are unpainted wood, bleached a similar gray-green by the summer sun and northern winter winds. The summer heat is relentless. There's no reliefs from the moment you open your eyes in the morning until you manage to fall asleep at night. Dust and dirt and turkey dung are everywhere.

The only critters that seemed to flourish were the tarantulas and the rattlesnakes. I only saw one tarantula, but it was disturbing enough to populate my bad dreams for the rest of the summer. Mother and Spotty became veteran snake killers. The hot air would carry the rasp of a large rattler, or sometimes a nest of two or three from one side of the yard to another. This would be punctuated by Mother's cries and the dog's barks. The snakes coiled to strike out at Mother and could leap out for several feet in this fashion.

Someone gave us a young Boston terrier we named Jigger because he would stand at the back door and beg to come in by crossing and uncrossing his front legs in a sort of dance. We had him a week before rattlesnakes appeared in the yard. Mother saw Spotty get bitten but in the rush of battle, but wasn't even aware that Jigger had been present. Both dogs were bitten. Jigger crawled off quietly and died while Mother was ministering to Spotty. The stalwart little terrier who had been my constant companion since my second Christmas was snake-bitten so frequently she eventually became immune to the venom.

We were beside ourselves with boredom. It was August. We had not been beyond our front gate since the Homecoming in late May. Desperate for something to do, I removed all the furniture from the bedroom at the end of the front screened porch, then swept the room and dusted the furniture before rearranging it in the room. Mother had to help me move the furniture and then make diplomatic suggestions regarding my furniture placement.

The next day Mother approached our father. "The children and I are going a little stir crazy here. Isn't there some place we could go as a family that isn't too expensive?"

Our father had been up working since dawn and was home for dinner and a nap. He rolled over and said, "Yes, you can come with me late this afternoon when I go feed the cattle on the lease."

It was a short drive, but it felt good nonetheless to be going somewhere. The cattle were scheduled to be fed bagged feed. The setting didn't seem right from the moment we arrived. The gate to the lease was at a corner of the property adjacent to another lease on the other side of the fence. The ground there was totally bare dirt, while there were still brown weeds on our side.

Our father pulled his truck up close to the troughs just a few hundred yards inside the gate and started honking his horn to call his cattle. He then began to pull fifty-pound bags of feed from the bed of the pickup and pour the contents into the troughs. Our cattle were not the only ones to appear.

There were a few starved creatures on the other side of the fence. Their owner had abandoned them. As they caught scent of the feed being poured into the troughs, the starving animals began throwing their bodies with what little strength they could muster against the barbed-wire fence. They were screaming rather than mooing, with their tongues extended and eyes bulging. They had eaten every blade of dead weed and thorny bush they could reach from their side of the fence.

Mother was speechless, while I jumped straight in, afire with righteous indignation, and demanded, "Who can we call to report this? Someone needs to help these animals. We can't let this go on."

Our father gave me a weary, indignant look and said, "Everyone in the county knows what that man is doing. That's his punishment." He finished feeding and we left. It was an awful ride home.

At some point in our childhood, between my fall in the alley in back of the Ellis Café and this feeding incident, our father began to assume that he couldn't take us anywhere without our misbehaving or causing a scene; but in this instance, I have to ask whose behavior was questionable. He had to have known what would happen in that pasture at feeding time. Why did he take us?

I have come to understand the behavior code subscribed to by my father and his peers. The Scots-Irish brought it with them from the Old World. Two of the main influences were vanity and secrecy and had developed as a result of living in constant poverty and the ensuing sense of shame. The questionable behavior of the absentee cattleman and the alcoholic store manager who lived in sin and beat his paramour's children were not reported to the proper authorities, who might lessen the suffering of either the children or animals, but they lost face with the rest of the men in the community.

From other bits and pieces I picked up during adolescence, I would realize this male-dominated society was founded on a strict double standard. All women were fair game. One social misstep by a girl could brand her unfavorably for life, while the same misbehavior added to the male's status with the other men. Some of the women were aware of this and ignored it. Others were totally clueless. Mother was among the latter.

I discovered this from a situation involving our father's uncle. T. C. Watts was a tall, good-looking man with sandy hair, blue eyes, and an outgoing personality. His first marriage lasted over 25 years, despite his active dating life. One of his later affairs, with the wife of the Sunday school superintendent, was so outrageous they even talked about it on the school bus.

Hard Times and Petty Crimes

Our cattle started looking skinny and acting starved in September, even though they were being regularly fed. Our father puzzled over this for several days. He finally set watch in the pasture late one night and saw Duval taking the feed out of the trough. He was selling it elsewhere. A day or so later Duval showed up in a rickety old vehicle, his entire family on board, for his paycheck.

It was the middle of the day. Our father was napping when they arrived. He went out to their ramshackle vehicle in his bare feet with his sleeveless T-shirt half tucked in his jeans and pitched a temper tantrum at Duval. I could hear the screaming from where I was hiding in the house. It was one of those times when the blood vessels in the side of his neck would bulge. He paid the hired hand and fired him. I was mortified that he did it in front of Duval's children.

Almost twenty-five years later, when Mother was dying, she mentioned in her matter-of-fact way that Duval had kept in touch with her for years after leaving our employ. Every time he had a fight with his wife and she had him thrown in jail or they had a baby or he changed jobs, Duval would call to keep Mother up to date. It was important to him for her to know where he was and what he was doing.

While our years in that unrecognized corner of Bastrop County were miserable, our lifestyle was light-years better than the existence Duval and his family led when they stayed in the hovel perched on the edge of Watts Lane. I'm not sure the house even had a front door. The opening faced the road, but I never got a good look because it was set back behind a pond with an outhouse perched on its bank.

Granny always made a big production of donating our outgrown clothes and her Sunday school literature to Duval's family. I knew all the literature that wasn't printed on slick paper would prove useful in the outhouse. But what would they do with our clothes? Granny always removed the zippers and buttons before passing them on. I doubted the Duvals had the knowledge or resources to replace the fasteners.

Our father bought Duval a raincoat one winter and a coat during another cold spell. The hired man wore them the day they were given to him but didn't have them the next time it rained or got cold. Our father made fun of the "useless Nigger" who couldn't keep up with his belongings. I suspect the clothing was sold out of desperation for food to feed their children.

Mother gave Duval the respect he deserved. Once he was gone, our isolation was complete. Granddaddy was dead. There was no one to drive down our rutted road to check on us now and again or anyone to stop once in a while to get a cold drink of water and share a moment or two of polite chitchat. We were alone.

Candid Snapshots

There were a number of snapshots taken of our family and the house on the Holcomb Place, but Mother was embarrassed about how we had lived and destroyed most of them. This one is of Joe and me with Jigger and Spotty and an anonymous cat. Jigger was a lovely animal who really danced when he wanted in the house. The environment was simply too harsh for him to survive. He wasn't savvy about living in the country and got too close to a rattlesnake.

Spotty is the white dog in the corner with her back to us. She joined our family when I was almost two and lived until my sophomore year in high school. The picture was probably taken to commemorate the arrival of the new Boston terrier, Jigger. Joe and Jigger are playing with the wheelbarrow while getting acquainted with each other. Joe was a beautiful child. Note his matching hat and gloves and how carefully his denim jacket is buttoned to the throat.

Mother wore glasses when she married our father in 1945. They were accidentally broken about the time Joe was born in 1949. She didn't have the money to replace them until the early 1960s, but we children always had what we needed, as well as a few extras like matching hat and gloves.

The background of this picture is more interesting than the fore. Note the bare dirt yard and the back of the house in the upper corner. That's the back porch and the rough steps leading up to it. The cistern is directly behind the porch, and the concrete pallet where the wringer washing machine stood is in the middle of the upper back.

This is the only picture we have of the house on the Holcomb property. No one lived in it again after we moved. Joe and Joy had the opportunity to visit it in the '70s, and this is the result. The drought of the 1950s is long over, and vegetation has grown waist high in the once-bare yard. The figure dressed in red on the left is my sister, Joy. The weeds are taller than her waist and hide the stilts that held the house off the ground. The screened porch was on the left with the main room in the middle. The two windows side-by-side on the other side of the house were in the kitchen. The one bare window on the second floor was covered by bare boards when we lived there. It's the loft or attic that Mother declared off limits for fear of snakes. The corrugated tin was nailed over the logs of the original one room cabin for additional insulation.

The Holcomb Place changed hands in the 1970s. The next owner divided the property into smaller lots and sold them, mostly to retirees from the Houston area. The county built another road providing access from a different side of the property. I can no longer point out the specific spot where our gate opened to the drive or where the mailbox stood.

Whoever bought the lot where the house stood torched it. The value of the antique logs, and handmade nails and bricks is questionable. Salvage would probably not have been cost-effective.

—CHAPTER TEN—

A Bitter Dose of Quinine

Wilma, our father's roan mare, wandered out on the Farm-to-Market Road one night and was hit and killed by a truck. It was a much simpler, less litigious time. The incident was considered a mere accident by everyone involved. Our father was faced with replacing his beloved horse for as little money as possible. He named the new mare Quinine, because she was a bitter dose to take.

A polite assessment of Quinine's personality would be that she was socially challenged. I came to realize after working with her for a couple of days that the horse was smart enough to do what was requested of her, but mean and spiteful and out to do me harm for the fun of it.

Quinine spent her summers in the field directly across the drive from the house where the pigs once resided. It was my responsibility to lead her each morning and evening to the stock tank to drink, and then back to the barn to feed her.

My bed on the screened porch was visible to the horse. She would hang as far as possible over the fence as soon as the sun rose and start making noises and kicking the dirt to get my attention. I would resist until the sun shining in my eyes and my conscience forced me to respond. I would go out to the field in my pajamas, put a halter around the horse's nose and lead her to the water tank.

The poor animal was so thirsty she usually raced me to the water. I would have to run to stay ahead of her to keep from getting knocked over. I'd sit on the bank and let her drink before leading her back to the barn where I put feed in the trough for her. Her pen included a big field for grazing, as well as the barn where she could retire to eat out of the trough and stay out of the sun. It was a simple assignment and would have been pleasurable, if the animal had been the least bit accommodating.

She considered any peaceful overtures I made towards her as opportunities to do me physical harm. She bit just hard enough to let me know she could really draw blood if she chose. I always went barefoot in the summer and suffered from an ingrown toenail on the big toe of my left foot. That was always the toe she stood on, while adding a final twist of her hoof and leg for good measure.

Once, early in our "relationship," Quinine made the mistake of letting me ride her without protest. We were in her pasture. I was riding bareback with only a rope halter. Admittedly, I got a little carried away and encouraged her to trot. Quinine took me up on the offer and galloped. She also chose the path and jumped over a short bush. It was the most exhilarating three seconds of my childhood. I loved it and couldn't understand why the horse wouldn't do it again. I now suspect she only jumped the bush because she thought I would fall off. It might have afforded her the opportunity to "accidentally" step on me again.

Quinine was an expert at avoiding my attempts to ride her. If I was able to get the rope halter on her at any time except feeding, she became adept at sidestepping my attempts to mount her. I didn't have a saddle and wouldn't have been able to lift one onto her back anyway. I had to lead her next to something close to her own height and climb on her from there. Her timing was perfect. She would stand exactly in the right spot while I scrambled on the taller object and then smoothly glide away, with a swat of her tail at an imaginary fly, just as I hung in the air. The way she scraped me off her back under low-hanging branches was probably classic material for a situation comedy, and would have been funny if it hadn't been so painful to my body and ego.

Our father had warned us to not spoil his horse and "make a fool" out of her. I would probably have spent more time with this animal, if she hadn't been so large and threatening. Other things also took place that summer that diverted my attention from that challenging personality.

Bubblegum Showdown

I tripped running up the back steps one evening and knocked the corner off my first permanent tooth in the resulting fall. The tooth became infected and had to be pulled, despite special treatments by a pediatric dentist. I was the first child in the third grade with a partial plate.

The continuing drought drained the meager resources of our community. The year I was in third grade, Floyd Martin, the shopkeeper-cum-school bus driver, started bringing a cigar box of penny candy and bubblegum on the bus every morning to sell on the drive into town. I was his best customer.

Despite my partial plate, bubblegum was always my choice from the cigar box. There's no doubt I probably sat in the middle of class, took out my partial plate along with a wad of gum, and untangled the two while the teacher was trying to hold our attention. My inability to stop chewing gum in school caused me to spend at least one or two recesses in front of a blackboard writing over and over "I will not chew gum in class." I secretly enjoyed the opportunity to write on the blackboard and practice my penmanship.

Our father was a newly elected member of the school board for the Bastrop Independent School District. Ruby Percy, my teacher, was a devoted educator who, no doubt, had contacted my parents regarding my disruptive behavior. One afternoon, our father was driving on a back gravel road and saw Floyd Martin coming towards him from the opposite direction. He flagged him down.

The two stopped with their pickup trucks parallel on the road and spoke through the open windows. "I want you to stop selling candy on the school bus in the mornings. It's causing Jackie Lee problems at school," our father demanded.

Mr. Martin paused for a moment to consider and then shook his head. "No, I don't see any reason to stop."

There was a significant pause while our father's quick temper flared. I saw it happen often enough to know his face grew red while the veins in the sides of his neck stood out. "Get out of the truck," he said.

Mr. Martin was smaller and older than our father. He also lacked the emotional involvement his opponent so readily displayed. There was no pause this time. "Okay, I'll stop."

Third grade presented a number of challenges besides forcing me to go "cold turkey" on my bubblegum habit. We were required to memorize the multiplication tables through twelve, the states and their capitals, the location of the major national parks, and to learn cursive writing. When it became apparent that I lacked the impetus to memorize the multiplication tables, our father handed down one of his edicts: "You have two weeks to memorize the multiplication tables or you won't be able to wear your wristwatch until the next marking period."

I walked around for fourteen days, clutching raggedy copies of the cursed math facts and muttering them under my breath. I was tested after supper on the appointed day. "All right," our father conceded. "You know your multiplication tables, but have you stopped biting your nails?"

I panicked. Of course I hadn't. That wasn't part of the bargain. It was only when Mother intervened to point this out that my wristwatch privileges were secured.

My Catholic Conversion

Despite my outlaw chewing-gum episode and the dreaded math, there was a bright spot in the third grade for me. A new girl joined our class that year. Julia Ann moved from a nearby parochial school and quickly became my best friend. We shared relatives from different sides of the family. My Great-Great-Uncle Lee was married to her Great-Aunt Julia. We had sleepovers at each other's houses, which was a first for me.

Julia was Catholic and taking religious education to make her first communion. She was a born teacher, and I was her first student. As we cuddled up together in her bed or mine, she would share with me her latest religion lesson. I think it was the story of Salome demanding the head of John the Baptist that sold me on Catholicism. I could understand a woman being so fearful of a man or so angry with him that she had to have him killed. It had more validity than the figure at our church of the Messiah who managed to run money changers out of the temple and live on insects and honey for forty days and nights in the desert and still remain perfectly coiffed and immaculate in attire.

The flaw in my religious conversion was my assumption that I had control of my spiritual life. My conception of place was also out of whack. The bus ride from my house to the school took at least a half-hour. The narrow road was cut through acres and acres of land clotted with mesquite trees. There were only a few clearings along the way. A couple of these held corncribs built from logs. I assumed I was being carried to a place where my parents were largely unknown. I knew I looked like everyone else in my family, but had no idea that most of the people in Bastrop had been well acquainted with my people for at least two or three generations. I didn't realize this recognition extended beyond the boundaries of Cedar Creek. I saw Bastrop as a big city far from home, where I was privileged to go every weekday to play with other children and read almost as much as I wanted. Math class was a small price to pay for the other delights.

On the basis of several extended whispered religious briefings with Julia, I considered myself a convert to Catholicism. My attendance at the Cedar Creek Protestant church was a minor detail in my nine-year-old mind.

Catholics were required to abstain from eating meat on Fridays. It was announced one Friday that the cafeteria had a limited number of fish servings available only to the

Catholic children. They were instructed to request fish at the steam table in the lunch line. I love fish. "I'm Catholic. May I please have a serving of fish?" I asked the woman behind the steam table. I thought she was going to drop her slotted spoon. "You're what?" the woman inquired, after getting a better grip on her utensil and her composure.

Her surprise was probably well-founded. There's no doubt she knew my family well enough to know they were devout Protestants. People living in a small town don't get out much. An innocent unexpected request such as mine could provide gossip fodder for at least a week. I enjoyed every bite of my fish and was totally clueless that my behavior had probably added yet another wrinkle to my already rumpled reputation.

Protected Environment?

Our father sold the A&A General Store in the spring after Granddaddy died. But Granny told Mother that J. A. Martin's father had T.B., and to keep us away from his store. I was instructed to continue to report to the A&A after school, with the warning that since we no longer owned the facility, I wouldn't have my usual after-school sandwich. "It will be tempting, but stay away from the candy counter and the cold cuts," Mother warned.

The new owner moved a bed into the back of the store behind the feed sacks and proceeded to make it his home. It was even more boring under his management than it had been under Granny's. Business declined. No one patronized the establishment or even stopped by now and again to visit. I got so bored one afternoon that I swept the rough wooden floor and cleared it of its medium-to-large dust bunnies. As I put the broom away, the owner opened the cash register and wordlessly handed me a quarter.

I displayed the magnificent sum at supper that night and described the unmade bed behind the feedbags. It was decided on the spot that from then on I was to report to J.A. Martin's to wait for our father after school.

Ambushed

Puberty grabbed hold of me during the summer between third and fourth grade. I had a major growth spurt and reached my full height. In the group shot of the fourth grade, I was the one in the back standing beside the teacher: a grown woman with a Buster Brown hair cut and Girl Scout shoes. I was lucky to be between home permanents when that shot was taken.

Our teacher had a family emergency early in the school year. Her husband, a local rancher, came into the classroom to give her a ride home. He stood in front of us and, with one hand holding his Stetson and the forefinger of the other hand pointing at us, said, "My wife has enough to worry about today with her sick momma. She doesn't have any time to be concerned about all of you. Don't let me hear that any of you misbehave today."

The substitute teacher was an illustrious pillar of the community. Her husband was the Superintendent of Schools. The class was working on long division. I didn't find math nearly as much fun as reading, and hoped if I ignored it long enough, it would go away. The substitute called me to the board to tackle a problem. When I proved to be clueless, she took the opportunity to let me and the rest of the class know how totally stupid I was. It doesn't take much to traumatize a kid already awkward and self-conscious about being strapped up to her chin by her first bra.

I did have one classmate who was willing to help me with math and keep me on track with our assignment, but she was Mexican. Mr. Floyd Martin made all the Mexican children ride in the back of the bus. I had to fight the older Caucasian kids for a seat close to the back for us to talk. It was a daily hassle.

It was no longer fun to ride the school bus. Jerry Mac had transferred to a high school in Austin. He didn't live in that district, but the administration admitted him without fanfare. Bastrop High was two-storied while the school in Austin was all on one level. It was a practical decision reached without a hearing or any paperwork. There was no more group singing on the afternoon ride home. It seemed shorter as I struggled with the politics of sitting close to the back of the bus and struggling to master a math fact without growing car sick. I've never been able to read in a moving vehicle without getting nauseous.

Boys and Girls Are Different

My brother Joe entered first grade the year I was in fourth. School started just after Labor Day. It was still as hot as midsummer. When we returned home at the end of the first day, Joe had his shoes and socks under his arm. He was more comfortable playing barefoot as we waited for the bus to pick us up for the ride home. Our father sternly warned him to keep his shoes on all day.

Joe was six. He either couldn't bear the temptation or he forgot his instructions. He made no pretense of hiding his dirty bare feet when we reached home that second afternoon. Our father beat Joe, swinging his doubled wide western belt as hard as he could, with the slight little boy begging, "Daddy, please don't hit me again." Joe was just a baby. How could a parent who supposedly loves his child lash out like that? I quickly learned it's much easier to be the target of punishment than to watch it happen to someone else.

Joe never learned to avoid our father. He worked hard to please him, but it seemed that the harder Joe tried, the more fault our father found with him. It has been my experience that there are fathers who are obnoxiously proud of their sons and live their lives vicariously through them, while some others may feel threatened by the presence of another male in the house.

Past Due Remuneration

Mother was good about keeping up with everyone in the family, as well as administering the family budget. She paid all the bills.

"You have been treating my child for almost three years now, and I've never had a bill despite numerous appeals. Please, we must pay you."

Mother made this request to both Dr. Tisdale and his office manager on a number of occasions before they finally complied. When the bill did arrive, Mother was terrified to open it. She carried it in her pocket all one day working up the courage to open it.

We had no money. Considering the time and effort the specialist had devoted to Joy, the sum should have been huge. When she did finally open the envelope, Mother found an itemized statement for all the supplies used during Joy's treatment: braces, casts, etc. There was no charge for professional services. Dr. Tisdale respected Mother's pride. There was no dollar amount we could have put on the gift he gave our family.

"Wet me go, wet me go, wet me go, Wover! Turn me Woose, what the use?" Joy was three and loved to sing this popular song, despite her minor difficulty with the letter "L." Our father called her "Tootie." The doctor decided the best treatment for her was to keep her in special shoes from morning to night and to carefully monitor her condition.

Thanks to Joy, our father's mother received a new title. To differentiate Granny from our great-grandmothers in conversation, she dubbed Granny "Plain Old Granny." Mother believed in being diplomatic and made her change it to "Plain Granny."

Family Legend or Tall Tale

J.C. Ellis, my paternal grandfather, is the man standing in the center of this group wearing the black hat and bowtie. Zula Watts Ellis, his wife is kneeling in front and holding their eldest son, J.C. Ellis, Jr. The man standing on the left wearing a white hat and bowtie is my grandfather's first cousin, Jim Ellis. Jim worked as a guard at Huntsville State Prison and visited central Texas when given time off from the prison.

This snapshot is a still from an early western silent movie. Jim Ellis is one the extras on horseback in the rear of the group. He's the only one looking into the camera rather than at the central characters. It's as though he's saying, "Can you believe I'm getting paid for this nonsense?" But I'm willing to bet he wouldn't have used the word nonsense.

When Jim Ellis came home to visit from Huntsville, he would stay with one relative or another out in the country. He loved to visit the bars on East Sixth Street in Austin. He'd catch a ride with someone in Cedar Creek who was going in to Austin and then hire a cab to bring him back.

One cab driver decided Jim was intoxicated enough to rob and tried to take his money when he dropped him off where he was staying. Jim's host was awakened to the sound of sporadic gunfire. He pulled his pants on under his night-shirt, slipped his bare feet in his boots and went outside to see what was happening.

He found Jim leaning against the hood of a cab. The driver was hiding behind a tree. Now and again, the cabbie would move from behind one tree to another, and Jim would take a shot at him.

"Jim," his host said, "you can't shoot that man."

"Aww, I'm just playing with him," Jim said. "If I wanted to kill him he'd already be dead."

Working as a prison guard hardens a man; he would play rough. I would not swear in court that this is a true story. There is no concrete documentation to support it, but I do believe something close to this did take place. It's just one of those family stories that gets handed down from one generation to the next. It also shows the attitude of our Scoti ancestry was still running strong and true in their twentieth century descendants.

Adios

"Ginny, please come here. I need you."

Mother was caught up in some task in the front of the house when our father called for help. She stepped out on the back porch to find him holding up one corner of it. The support had given way, and the back porch was about to fall off the house. Our family had to find another house. This one was falling down around us. It was also too small to accommodate our growing family. Mother was preg-nant again.

Our father's Uncle Elmo, who owned the family-style café in Austin, had recently decided to retire. His only son had been killed in World War II. Our father was his closest relative in the next generation. Uncle Elmo offered to swap some land and cattle for the café. Our parents decided that Mother would run the café while our father would work as a cattle buyer for a meat-packing plant. The café had a small apartment across the back alley where our parents and Joe would sleep. There was a bedroom and bath attached to the back of the café for Joy and me.

In the weeks leading up to the move, I resolved to re-form and even read an etiquette book from cover to cover. I felt confident I would know what to do with a finger bowl, should I ever encounter one. We packed our few belongings and left the Holcomb Place in August of 1957.

When they had taken possession of this property, our parents were young and hopeful and energetic. While we lived there, Mother proved herself capable of assuming responsibility for major tasks and making them a financial success. Our father convinced us and the community that he was a hard-working, honest man. The pattern they had established in their marriage was set in the Scots-Irish tradition of pride and stubbornness, secrecy and violence. Mother was determined to make her marriage appear a success. Our father had a charming face he wore in public to cover the temper beneath.

A neighbor volunteered to drive Joe and Joy and me to our new place in Austin. He stopped the car at the far end of the barn from the house and had us turn back for one more look. It was late in the day. There was a fine mist of dust from the vehicles that had just pulled away. The combination of dust and fading light softened the imperfections of the bedraggled log cabin and gave it an almost mythical appearance.

This proved to be my last glimpse of our former home. I never had the opportunity to visit there again, but it doesn't really matter. A piece of my heart never left.

Reputation Remains

This is the teacher who left school to nurse her sick mother. At the time she seemed ancient; but was probably not even middle-aged. I'm the girl under straight bangs with her eyes closed beside the teacher. I was terminally self-conscious at the time and saw myself as big as a cow. Now I see I wasn't even the tallest girl in the class.

I don't remember many of the names of my former classmates, but have carried fragments of their life stories with me all my life. The mother of the Brownie i n the front row was widowed early and ran a beauty shop out of her home to support her family. The second boy in the row in front of me was the son of the local grocer. Next to him stands the son of two teachers. One of the Mexican boys didn't write fluent English and routinely copied my classwork. Another boy graduated with the class and moved to California. He returned for the 25th reunion and confided in one of his classmates that he'd never come back. There were too many depressing old people in the class.

This picture was probably taken on a Thursday or Friday in the fall before a football game. One of the girls has a spirit ribbon pinned to the front of her dress. I believe she's also the one who helped me with math on the bus ride home from school. I understand she grew up to work for the IRS. The girl next to her is the one who converted me to Catholicism. She spent her life teaching pre-first and first grade, and remains a heart-of-my-heart friend.

I've never been included in any of the class reunions in Bastrop because I didn't graduate with them, but a couple of times I have met two or three on a casual basis. Despite their valiant efforts to be diplomatic, the truth has a way of coming out. My memory may have distorted the ages of my teachers, but I was just as rambunctious and as big a messy handful as I recalled.